Acknowledgements
The photographs on p. 80 bottom right and p. 89 top right
appear by courtesy of Kodak Ltd.

Published 1975 by
The Hamlyn Publishing Group Limited
London · New York · Sydney · Toronto
Astronaut House, Feltham, Middlesex, England
© 1975 The Hamlyn Publishing Group Limited

ISBN 0 600 30206 7

Printed in the Canary Islands (Spain) by
Litografia A. Romero S.A.
D. L. TF. 1113 - 1974

Answer Book of
SCIENCE

Susan Baker

HAMLYN
London · New York · Sydney · Toronto

Contents

What makes the Sun shine?

The Sun is a vast, fiery sphere of glowing gas at the centre of our solar system. The centre of the Sun is very, very hot. The temperature is about 13,000,000°C, because a *thermonuclear reaction* is continually taking place within it. In this reaction, the hydrogen gas of which the Sun is almost entirely made, is converted into another gas, helium. During this reaction, enormous amounts of nuclear energy are released. Some of this energy reaches our planet in the form of heat and light. We call it sunshine.

Without sunshine, people could not survive on the Earth. It provides us with all our food and heat.

People need food to stay alive and give them energy. Their meat comes from animals, the animals eat plants and the plants need sunshine to enable them to convert water and carbon dioxide into their food, sugar, by a process called *photosynthesis*.

Heat comes from fuels such as coal and oil. Coal is the remains of prehistoric plants; oil is formed from the remains of living creatures. Without sunshine, these plants and animals would never have existed. Millions of years from now, the Sun may stop shining. Life on Earth as we know it, will then cease.

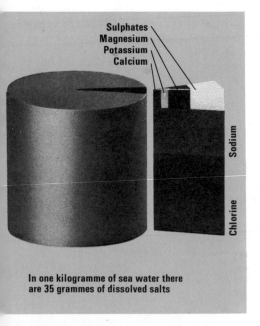

In one kilogramme of sea water there are 35 grammes of dissolved salts

Why is the sea salty?

If you leave a bowl of salty water in a sunny place for a few days, the water will gradually dry up, or evaporate. As the water slowly disappears, it will taste more and more salty, until it dries up completely leaving white, crusty crystals.

This is what has been happening to the sea for millions of years. The water evaporates off the sea, is blown inland as clouds, falls as rain and then runs down to the sea again, carrying more salts with it. These have been dissolved out of the rocks and soil that the water seeps through.

There are about twenty-five grammes of salt in every litre of sea water. How did so much salt get into the sea? One theory is that during the millions of years that there has been water on Earth, huge quantities of brine, that is, salt dissolved in water, have poured out of cracks in the Earth's crust, during underwater earthquakes or volcanic eruptions.

In some of the enclosed, shallow seas, such as the Mediterranean, and the Caribbean, there is a much higher concentration of salt.

ORBITAL MOTIONS IN WAVES

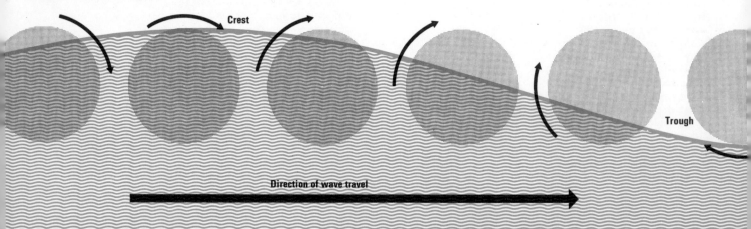

Where do waves come from?

If you drop a stone in a still pond of water, circles or ripples, or waves, start to move outwards from the point where the stone hit the water. It looks as if the water itself is moving outwards, but in fact it is only a wave of energy that moves through the water, causing it to rise and fall evenly.

We call the top of a wave its peak, or more correctly, its *crest*, while the lowest point the water falls to between two crests, is called a *trough*. The series of waves, caused by a stone dropping in this case, is called a *wave train*, and the first crest which travels forward is called the *wave front*.

On the sea, the wind blows on the water, trying to blow it about like sand. But the water is pulled back down towards the Earth by the force of gravity. The continual lifting and dropping causes waves to start up and these can grow huge if the wind continues to blow hard.

Huge tidal waves, called by the Japanese name *tsunami*, are caused by violent shocks in the water when a seaquake occurs. Tsunami are very dangerous, sweeping over and destroying everything in their path as they can travel at up to 700 k.p.h.

Why do boats bob on the sea?

If you watch a small boat, or a seagull, or a piece of driftwood floating on the sea, you will notice that although it bobs about, it always stays in roughly the same place, as if it were anchored to the sea-bed. As each wave rolls in beneath it, the boat rises up on the *crest*, rides forward just a little, and then drops into the *trough* of the wave and floats back to its original position.

For a boat, or a gull, this must feel like going for a ride on the big wheel at a fairground (fortunately the waves are not usually so large). The boat does not get swept along by the waves because the water itself does not move very far. Only the *force* which causes the waves travels through the water.

When the waves come near to the shore where the water is shallower, the waves break. This is because the water is not deep enough for it to move in a circle. The crests of the waves become top-heavy, break off, and stream down into the trough in a white foam. It is these *breakers* that are so excellent for surfing. The surfboard rides forward on the continuously breaking wave.

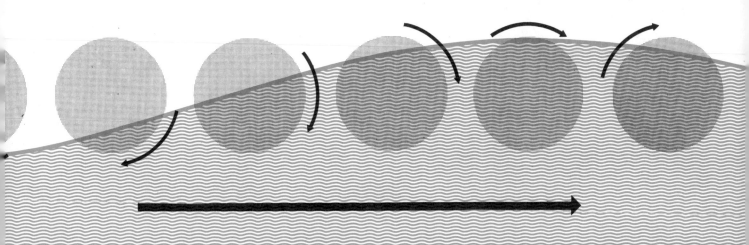

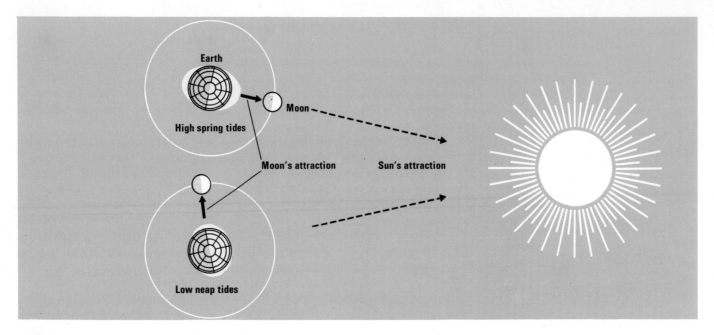

Earth

Moon

High spring tides

Moon's attraction   Sun's attraction

Low neap tides

What causes the tides?

Twice every day, the surface of the sea rises and falls. This causes an ebb and flow of currents in the water. This effect is commonly known as the tide.

The tide is caused by the gravitational pull of the Moon on the Earth. All bodies exert a mutual force of attraction on each other, according to the law of gravity. For example, the Earth holds the satellite Moon in its orbit around the Earth. In its turn, the Earth is

attracted towards the Moon as it moves round. Only the waters on the Earth's surface are free to actually move, and the water rises up at the point on Earth directly facing the Moon at any one time.

The waters also rise up on the opposite side of the Earth because they are effectively 'left behind'. This is because they are attracted less strongly, since they are further away from the Moon.

The distance of the Moon from the Earth varies slightly, and its path around the Earth changes.

At most places along the shores, there are two daily tides. One is when the Moon is directly overhead and the other is when it is on the opposite side of the Earth. High tide each following day is over an hour later.

Twice a year, when the Moon is closest to the Earth, there are high tides, known as spring tides.

What makes sea caves form?

Along some coastlines, the shoreline consists of rocky cliffs. These are continuously being pounded by the waves, especially in stormy winter weather, when the sea is exceptionally rough.

Near the shore, the waves tend to scoop up sand and stones and these are hurled at the cliffs, especially near their base.

Gradually the cliffs are worn away at the bottom. The overhanging part tends to fall, so the sea has managed to push the coastline back by a few metres, and the process starts again.

Where the cliffs are made of hard rock, the sea usually manages to find a few places where the rock is weaker than the rest. This is sometimes where an underground stream comes out through a crack in the rock. These wear away more quickly and the sea swirls in with extra force and scours out small caves. As the cave grows larger the force of the waves rushing into it is all the greater for being trapped in a small space. Sometimes you can hear water pounding beneath you in a cave, when you are walking along a cliff top.

How were the mountains made?

Early geologists often found the skeletons or fossils of millions of tiny sea creatures at the tops of some mountains. This showed that the rocks must once have lain on the seabed. This type of rock is called sedimentary rock. It is made up of millions of tonnes of sediment, or particles of rock, eroded by Sun, wind, rain and frost and washed down by the rivers from the mountains to the sea. There it settled on the bottom of the sea, becoming sandwiched between layers of the tiny skeletons, and eventually it all became compressed into rock.

It was the weight of the sediment on the seabed that disturbed the balanced forces in the Earth's crust and caused a great upheaval. The eroded mountains collapsed and folded underneath the layers of sediment, which themselves were folded and forced up into mountain folds.

Limestone and sandstone are sedimentary rocks and are eroded away relatively quickly. Mountains in limestone and sandstone regions often have queer distorted shapes because of this.

The folding and crushing that takes place during mountain building produces great heat and this changes, or metamorphoses, some of the rock. Marble and slate are metamorphic rocks. Much of the Alps in Europe are metamorphic. Their sharp, jagged appearance, caused by frost shattering and erosion show that they are relatively young, for they have not yet been worn smooth.

Some of the oldest mountains are made of hard igneous rock, such as granite, which was once molten in the Earth's interior. They usually have a smooth, rounded shape as they are worn down very slowly.

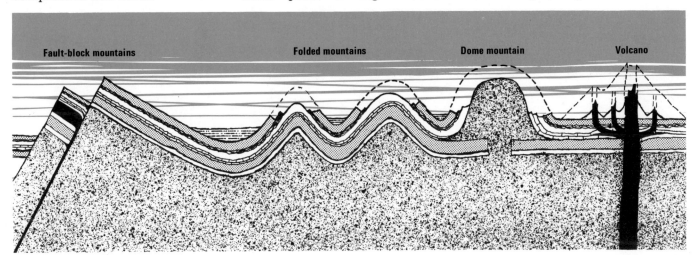

Fault-block mountains   Folded mountains   Dome mountain   Volcano

What is the inside of the Earth like?

The heart of our planet Earth is made of a very dense metallic material. Around this is a molten mass containing iron and nickel. Together these make up the *core* of the Earth, which is roughly a sphere about 7,000 kilometres in diameter.

The core of the Earth is surrounded by an extremely dense layer of partly molten rock called the *mantle*. It is about 3,000 kilometres thick.

During earthquakes, molten rock from the *sima* or *magma* escapes to the surface through cracks and fissures in the *sial* above.

The sial and the sima make up the outermost layer of the Earth called the *crust*. This is as thin as five kilometres in some places and is nowhere more than about a hundredth of the thickness of the mantle.

The crust is thinnest under the oceans where there is only a layer of sima. The sial only covers the land masses. The boundary between the surfaces of the crust and the mantle is known as the *Mohorovicic discontinuity*. There have been attempts to drill through the crust to reach the mantle and obtain samples. The drilling has taken place under the Pacific Ocean. So far it has not been very successful.

We have learnt about the composition of the crust through excavations in mines, caves and quarries. Volcanoes pour out molten material from deeper parts of the Earth and geologists are always quick to obtain samples of these for analysis.

Earthquakes cause shock waves which travel right through the Earth and provide a means for finding out more about the material inside.

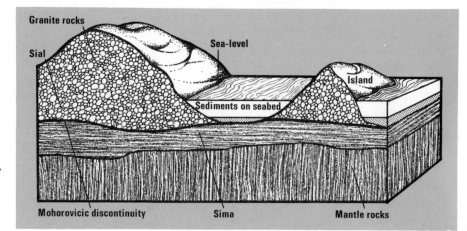

Granite rocks · Sial · Sea-level · Island · Sediments on seabed · Mohorovicic discontinuity · Sima · Mantle rocks

Why do volcanoes erupt?

It is the molten rock and gases that churn away under the Earth's crust until they find a weak fault or fissure through which to escape that makes volcanoes erupt. Then they force their way through, building up more pressure, until they erupt, often noisily and violently, onto the surface. Huge jets of steam rush up into the air, disturbing the atmosphere and causing storms. The jets carry mineral-laden gases and clouds of hot ash which rain down all around. Out of the crack, or vent, molten rock pours and flows downhill. We call this a *lava flow*. Successive eruptions build up a volcano cone. If the top of the volcano is blown away, the cavity is called a *caldera*.

If this molten rock, or *magma*, is a very stiff fluid, it often causes the most violent eruptions. Because it flows more slowly, more pressure is built up, and sometimes the magma at the surface solidifies to form a hard plug. Eventually the pressure becomes great enough to blow out the plug and the resulting explosion is extremely violent. Such an eruption wrecked the town of St. Pierre in Martinique, when the nearby Mont Pelée erupted in 1902.

In the Pacific there are many islands that are the tops of huge dome-shaped *shield* volcanoes. These erupt less violently, causing a gentle flow of lava. The reason for the difference in behaviour is that the magma is more liquid and contains less gas. Great pressure, therefore, does not build up.

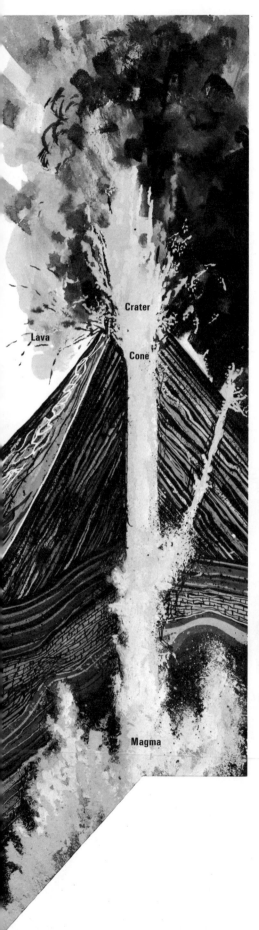

Lava

Crater

Cone

Magma

How does a glacier move?

If you are ever in the mountains, find a good viewpoint to look down the length of a valley. If the mountainsides slope down gradually to form a V shape, there is probably a stream or fast-flowing young river cutting its way downhill. But if the valley's sides are very steep, possibly even vertical, yet curved at the bottom where they join the valley floor, you are looking at a U-shaped valley, formed by a glacier. The glacier, a huge river of ice, may have long since melted away, or it may have receded back up the mountain. If it still exists, you will see a rushing river of icy, grey melt-water. The river flows out continuously from under the *snout* at the end of the glacier.

Not only the river flows down the mountain. The whole river of ice is flowing too, although it may advance only a few metres a year.

The centre part of the glacier flows fastest, while at the sides the ice drags against the valley walls, scouring them out. Over thousands of years a deep U-shaped valley is cut into the mountain.

The ice grinds the rock away to a fine powder and it is this that causes the glacier melt-water to look milky. The scouring action of the ice is increased by all the loose rocks and stones that are carried along beneath it. Where these are deposited, in great untidy heaps. they are called *moraine*.

The ice is like a solid, glassy sheet. Where it bends, on the outside corners and just before steep drops, the ice cracks and deep *crevasses* open up. These tend to close up in winter and open more in summer. Similarly, the glacier shrinks a little in summer as it melts, and grows in winter. If it shrinks more than it grows, we say it is receding. At present, most of the world's glaciers are receding.

How do small streams grow into big rivers?

A river passes through three stages in its life: youth, maturity and old age.

Particles of soil and rock gradually wear away a channel, as rain falling on mountains seeps through the soil. A little gorge may then be cut when the stream joins other streams. Zig-zag courses are made by these small rivers on hillsides when they change direction to avoid obstructions.

Over the years a river gradually cuts down the hillside, levelling off the slope. It may also cut back into the hill cutting into another little valley.

The mature river soon stops avoiding obstacles. Instead it flows past them, silting them up and eventually flowing over them.

The land alongside it may become silted up and flattened. This is a flood plain and the river is now in old age, deep, broad and full. It meanders or winds across the flood plain, depositing debris at the bends. Some bends are by-passed leaving *ox-bow lakes*, while the rest of the debris is deposited as a *delta*, where the river meets a lake or the sea.

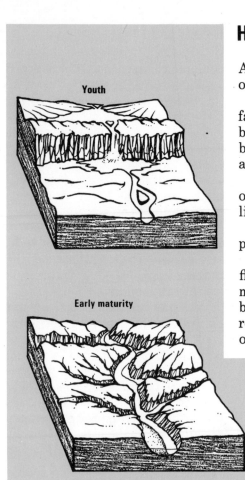

Youth

Early maturity

Late maturity

Old age

How are caves formed?

Most caves are the site of dried-up underground watercourses. They are usually found in hillsides of soft rock, such as limestone, which has been dissolved away by centuries of flowing water.

Caves are found where underground rivers come out at the surface. These rivers can sometimes be traced back through a whole system of caves. This may lead to a huge, deep pot-hole or shallow hole where a river has found its way underground through a fault or crack.

14

What are stalactites?

Stalactites are the stony 'icicles' found hanging from the roofs of limestone caves. Beneath a stalactite there may be a *stalagmite*, growing upwards from the cave floor.

They are both made of calcium carbonate. This is the mineral that is dissolved out of limestone by water flowing over it. Where the water drips slowly from the roofs of caves, it leaves the chalky particles behind. These slowly grow into the long, pointed stalactites and stalagmites. Where they are undisturbed for a great many years, these may grow to enormous lengths.

Why does frozen water make pipes burst?

Most things shrink, or *contract*, as they get colder, but water is strange, as we shall see in later pages. It contracts until its temperature falls to 4°C. Then it starts to *expand*, or get larger again as it gets still colder.

At 0°C water turns to ice. So a piece of ice takes up more space than the cold water it was made from. You can see this for yourself if you freeze some water in the refrigerator.

In frozen water pipes, the metal shrinks while the frozen water expands. The pipes then often crack under the strain. When the ice melts, water leaks from the cracks.

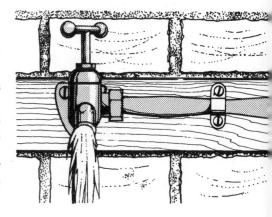

How do fish survive in frozen ponds?

Even in the hardest winters, fish and other animals living in deep ponds usually survive. This may seem surprising when there is a very thick layer of ice completely covering the surface.

They manage to survive because the water freezes from the surface downwards and in deep ponds there is unfrozen water at the bottom.

Usually, when a substance is heated, it gets larger, or expands, and grows lighter. When it cools, it shrinks or contracts, becoming heavier, or more *dense*. But water behaves in an unusual manner. If you put a pan of water on a hotplate you can see that the hot water rises to the top as it expands, and the cold water sinks to the bottom because it is heavier. But when water is cooled down, it only gets heavier until its temperature reaches four degrees above freezing point. Then, surprisingly, it begins to expand again, however far the temperature falls. So, as ice at 0°C is lighter than water at 4°C, the ice floats above the water. The thick coating of ice prevents the water from getting any colder, so the fish remain safe until the ice melts.

Why don't oil and water mix?

If you pour oil onto water, the mixture doesn't swirl into clouds like other liquids, such as fruit juice or milk. Instead the oil runs through the water in globules, rounded droplets, or ropy strands. These eventually join up again and the oil and water separate out as two distinct layers. Most cooking oils will float on the surface of water because they have a lower density than water; that is they are lighter.

Because they do not mix, oil is said to be immiscible with water. Two miscible liquids would be two that mix completely to form a homogeneous *mixture*.

A homogenous mixture is one that is of the same composition right through. Milk that is homogenized is milk that has been treated so that the cream and fats are mixed right through it so that no cream floats on 'top of the milk'.

Oil and water do not mix because the attraction of the oil molecules to each other is far greater than their attraction to water molecules. This involves the phenomenon known as surface tension.

Oils are used for water-proofing articles in such forms as varnish, polish and leather dressing. Some oils dissolve in alcohol and are used in the manufacture of perfume and flavourings.

Why are snowflakes all different?

Snowflakes look beautiful if examined through a microscope, when their hexagonal (six-sided) structures can be clearly seen.

One snowflake may be made up of fifty or more interlocked crystals, forming an intricate pattern with fern-like arms. It is unlikely that with so many possible combinations of crystals, any two snowflakes should be alike.

However, the overall form and structure may be similar for snowflakes which fall together. For they were formed under the same set of conditions, at the same temperature, from the same amount of water vapour, and so on. These conditions will determine whether the snowflakes form as needles or as plates.

What do we mean by the snow line?

In some parts of the world there are permanent snowfields. In the Arctic regions at the poles, these reach down to sea-level; in Greenland they are less than 2 kilometres above sea-level; in the Rockies they are at 3 kilometres and in the Alps at 2 kilometres above sea-level.

The height of the snow line depends on the height of the Sun, the wind, temperature and humidity. The line rises in summer and sometimes it even changes from year to year.

Did you know that there are even permanent snowfields at the equator? Some of the huge mountains, such as Kilimanjaro in Africa, rise above the permanent snowline.

How are snowflakes made?

Snow is a solid form of water that grows in the atmosphere when it is very cold and falls to Earth in the form of snowflakes.

Only one-third of the Earth's surface normally has any snow. It can come from frozen water vapour in a cloud, or even from a cloudless sky, if it contains some water vapour at a low temperature. The vapour condenses at a temperature below the freezing point.

The water forms crystals that interlock to form six-sided patterns. These may form into flat, plate-like flakes, or stack together to form needle-like flakes. Under severe conditions they may pack together into hard pellets.

What is dew?

Dew is the name for the drops of water you see sparkling on the grass, decorating spiders' webs early in the morning.

Quite quickly, warm sunshine dries the dew off. Even if the Sun hardly shines at all, the temperature rises, and the warmth makes the water *evaporate*. But as soon as the Sun goes down, the air temperature drops and the dew falls again.

The air cannot hold all the moisture at a low temperature and the moisture, or water vapour, *condenses*, turning back into water droplets.

The amount of moisture in the atmosphere is known as the *humidity*. When the weather is very humid, it feels hot and sticky.

When it is very cold, the dew freezes. It is then called frost. The dew is often heaviest in the early autumn when the difference between the day and night temperature is greatest.

How does a siphon work?

Water always flows downhill. So how is it possible to make water flow up a pipe? You can do this yourself if you make a siphon from a piece of rubber tubing or a bent pipe.

Dip a flexible tube well under the surface of the water in a reservoir, and suck the tube carefully. After all the air is sucked out, water will come up the tube too. It will continue to flow out of the tube if the mouth of the tube is held below the level of the water surface in the reservoir.

The water flows up the pipe in the first place because by sucking out the air the pressure is reduced. It will continue to flow until the pressure at both surfaces is the same.

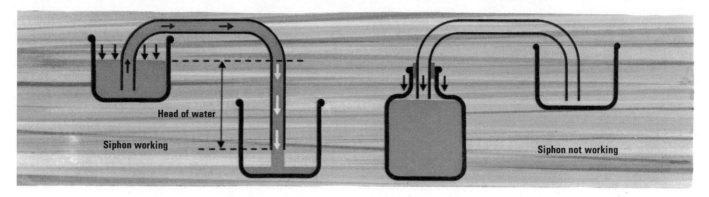

Head of water

Siphon working

Siphon not working

Where does rain come from?

Rain comes from the dark coloured clouds we call *nimbostratus* when they form in flat layers, and *cumulonimbus* if they are high banks of fluffy clouds.

The clouds contain condensed water vapour which has been evaporated by the heat of the Sun and has risen on air currents. The vapour condenses as it cools, and when the drops of water grow too big and heavy they fall, or are *precipitated*, as rain.

Rainfall often occurs where clouds blow into high land and are forced to rise into the colder air, higher in the atmosphere.

Apart from a drop in temperature, a drop in pressure can also cause rain to fall. The low pressure zone of the atmosphere, called a depression, cannot support the weight of the clouds of water droplets.

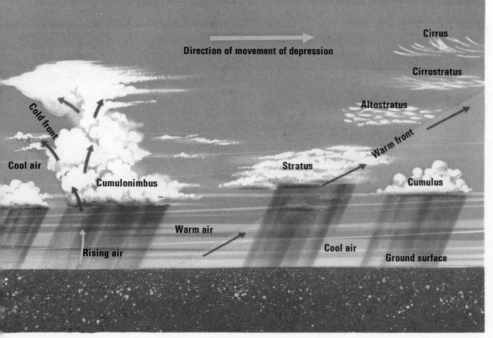

Direction of movement of depression

Cirrus

Cirrostratus

Altostratus

Cold front

Warm front

Cool air

Stratus

Cumulus

Cumulonimbus

Warm air

Rising air

Cool air

Ground surface

Left; We can learn a lot about the weather in store for us, by studying the clouds. The soft, wispy ones high in the sky are cirrus, and stratus can be seen on very grey days. The dark clouds (cumulonimbus) bring us rain and cumulus are the 'cotton wool' clouds.

Why does it rain more on high ground than on low?

The water on the Earth is being continuously recycled. The hot Sun makes the water evaporate from the sea and it rises to form clouds. These are blown inland by the wind until they reach high ground, such as a range of hills or mountains. Here, currents of air make the clouds rise higher into the atmosphere where it is colder.

The cold causes the clouds of water vapour to condense and fall as rain, often on the seaward side of mountain ranges. The rain seeps through the ground, running downhill in streams, or underground rivers. These join other streams to make rivers, which eventually flow back into the sea, or into great lakes.

There the Sun starts the evaporation process again, and rainclouds form to begin their journey to the mountains.

Rain will fall as soon as the clouds are cooled. As the air gets cooler higher up, it naturally tends to rain on high ground first.

Below: In this picture we can see how the water cycle works. Water evaporates from the sea and is carried inland by the wind in the form of clouds. Water also evaporates from rivers, the land surface and vegetation. As it rises, the vapour forms clouds. These grow cooler in the sky and then condense, and rain, sleet, snow or hail falls, finding a way back to the rivers and the sea.

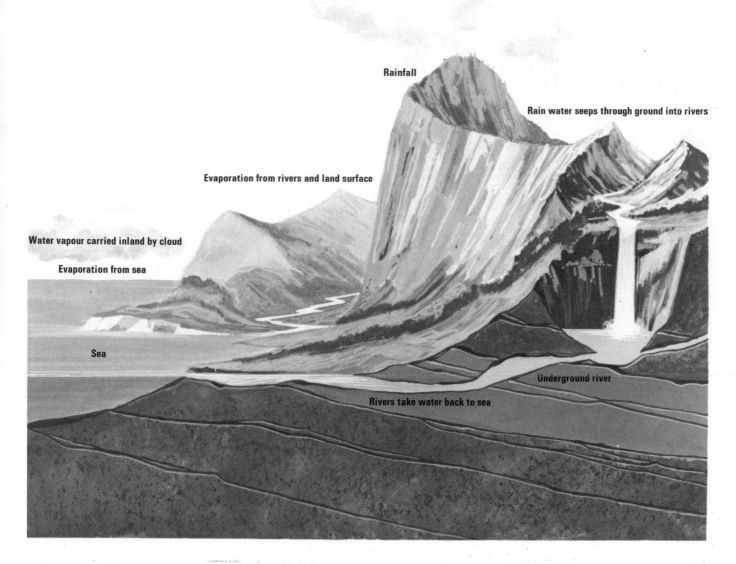

Rainfall

Rain water seeps through ground into rivers

Evaporation from rivers and land surface

Water vapour carried inland by cloud

Evaporation from sea

Sea

Underground river

Rivers take water back to sea

What is surface tension?

Although a liquid, such as water moves about freely, spreading everywhere, it still tends to 'stick to itself' rather than to the surface it touches.

Within the liquid, every bit, or *molecule*, of liquid holds on to all the other molecules of liquid around it. The molecules at the surface only have other liquid molecules on one side of them, so they hold on to these doubly hard. This sets up a strain in the surface which behaves rather like an elastic skin, such as on a balloon. This effect is known as *surface tension*.

You can see the effect of surface tension when you fill a glass of water to the brim. The water actually bulges over the top slightly, and the 'skin' stretches down to meet the sides and hold it in the glass.

Drops of water on a smooth surface show the same effect. The water surface is under tension, or strain, and tends to shrink as small as possible, producing a tight, bulging drop of water.

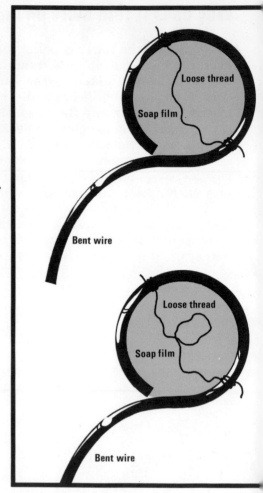

Right: You can do this experiment to test surface tension. Firstly tie a piece of thread loosely across a wire ring. A film will form if the wire is dipped in a soap solution. If half the soap film is broken the thread will become taut by the surface tension in the remaining film. Now try the experiment with a loop formed in the thread.

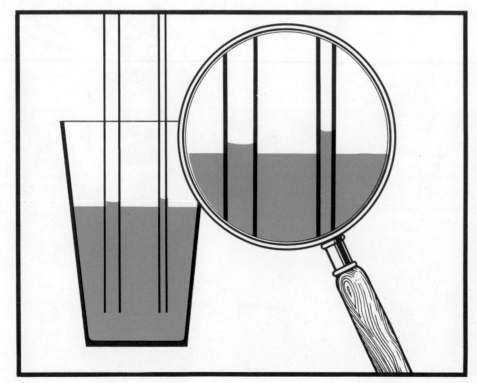

What makes water rise up narrow tubes?

The molecules within a liquid pull others at the surface inwards, producing surface tension. In a narrow tube, the liquid near the walls is only pulled by water on one side of it. This means that the surface by the wall is not pulled as tight as the liquid surface at the centre of the tube. As a result, the surface of the column of liquid is curved, the centre being pulled down further than the sides.

The sloping liquid surface, where it meets the walls of the container, is called the *meniscus*.

In narrow tubes, the force of the surface tension is enough to pull up a drop of water as the strain tries to make the surface

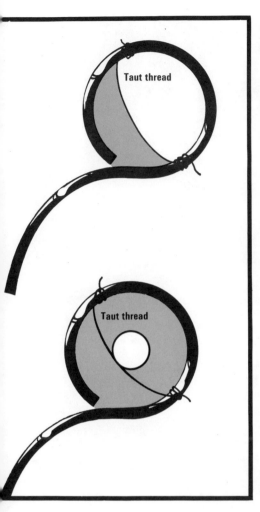

Taut thread

Taut thread

How does a lift pump work?

Nature tries to make all pressures equal everywhere. Men make use of this fact to make a lift pump to draw water easily. You could easily make a pump like the one in the picture for yourself.

A lift pump is a cylinder with a stopper at the bottom and a piston at the top, each containing a valve.

At the first downstroke of the piston, air rushes out of the top valve. At the next upstroke, the top valve closes and water rushes in through the bottom valve, filling the space beneath the piston. At the next downstroke, the piston compresses the water in the cylinder which closes the bottom valve. To release the pressure, the water rushes out at the top.

By pumping the piston up and down for several strokes, enough pressure can be built up to keep a steady flow of water gushing out of the top.

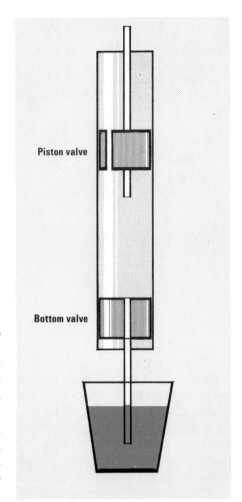

Piston valve

Bottom valve

shrink. Gradually the water creeps up the tube. This effect is called *capillarity*. The narrower the tube, the higher the liquid rises. Very narrow tubes are called capillary tubes.

Plants draw water up through their roots and stems by capillary action. Cork, sponges and blotting paper become saturated in the same way.

You can see this for yourself by setting up the experiment seen in the picture on the left. Fill a glass with orange juice (or any other coloured liquid for that matter). Put two plastic straws in the glass, one thick and one thin. The liquid will rise higher in the thin straw.

How does an insect walk on water?

Some insects can run across the surface of a pond without sinking. One of the most obvious is the water boatman.

This has quite a small body, but four of its legs are very long. These enable it to spread its small weight over a large area of the surface. The 'skin' of the water is able to support the very slight weight of each of the insect's feet.

The 'skin' on the water is produced by surface tension.

The insect moves in quick darts, never jumping high off the water surface and always landing on all four feet at the same time. In this way it never lands with enough force to break the surface tension.

Why do some things float and others sink?

Whether an object will float in a liquid, or sink, depends on its *density* compared with the density of the liquid. If the density of the object is less than the density of the liquid it will float; if it is greater, it will sink.

Density is a measure of the amount of matter in a certain volume of a substance.

A volume of one cubic centimetre (c.c.) of water weighs one gram. We say that the density of water is one gram per c.c. The density of lead is 11·3 grams per c.c., which is so much greater than that of water, that almost anything made of lead will undoubtedly sink.

Cork, balsa wood and expanded polystyrene all float in water because they have a very low density. This is partly because of the large amount of air that is trapped between the fibres of these materials.

Huge ships also have a lot of air trapped in the compartments in the hull. So, although a lump of steel would sink, the overall density of a ship is low enough for it to float.

Why does cream float best on coffee with sugar in it?

If two liquids of different densities are poured together, the one with the lower density will float to the surface and form a separate layer. Light oil floats on water and cream will float on milk if it is left standing.

You may have noticed that cream will not float on hot coffee. But if you stir sugar into the coffee first, the cream will float, if you pour it carefully. You can actually see it rising to the surface. This is because, by adding sugar, the density of the coffee is increased. The density of the cream is unchanged, but it is *relatively* less dense, so it floats more easily.

You may have found that it is rather easier to swim in sea water than in fresh water, especially if it is a very salty sea like the Mediterranean. In fact, photographs have been taken of people reading as they float in the Dead Sea! This is because it is easier to float in salt water as the salt makes the sea more dense than fresh water.

Who was Archimedes?

Archimedes was a Greek who lived from about 287 to 212 B.C. He was a scientist, and studied many of the laws of physics, including the behaviour of levers. But he is probably best remembered for his study of *flotation* and for his law governing floating bodies, known as Archimedes' Principle.

This principle states that when an object is floating in a liquid, the upthrust is equal to the weight of the liquid displaced.

The *upthrust* on a body is the amount of support it receives from the liquid, or its apparent loss in weight. An object feels lighter if you hold it under water. When it floats, the upthrust is equal to its whole weight.

The weight of liquid displaced is the weight of the amount of water that is pushed aside by the object. A block of light wood may float right on the surface of a water tank, hardly displacing any water. A large, heavy block may float almost submerged. Then it will displace a volume of water equal to its own volume. A rise in the water level seen on the sides of the tank will show this.

The density of an object can be measured by using Archimedes' Principle. There is a legendary story of how Archimedes himself is supposed to have used this method to find out if the gold in the king's crown was pure, or partly fake.

Below: Archimedes discovered his theory of flotation as he was getting into his bath one day. He was so excited that he shouted *Eureka* (I have found it).

How can a solid, a liquid and a gas be made of the same kind of material?

Solid

Ice, water and steam are a solid, a liquid and a gas respectively, and all have the same chemical composition. In each case the matter is in a different state.

Any substance, such as water, is made up of millions of identical molecules. In the solid state, when water is called ice, these molecules are held quite firmly together. The molecules do move, or *vibrate*, a little, but they tend to form a solid shape.

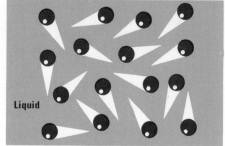

Liquid

If the solid is heated up, the molecules vibrate faster and more energetically. As the molecules move further apart, the object grows bigger, or expands. With further heating the molecules break away from each other, the solid loses its shape and starts to flow. It has *melted* to change to a liquid.

Yet more heat will make the liquid *boil* and it will finally begin to *evaporate*, changing to a gas. As a liquid, the molecules could move about freely but were still bound to each other. In changing to a gas, by vibrating even more quickly, they have broken free altogether and tend to expand and disperse in the atmosphere. All these changes that have taken place are physical changes. There has been no change in the chemical composition of the substance, although its appearance has changed.

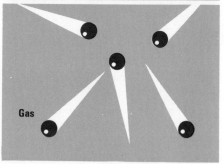

Gas

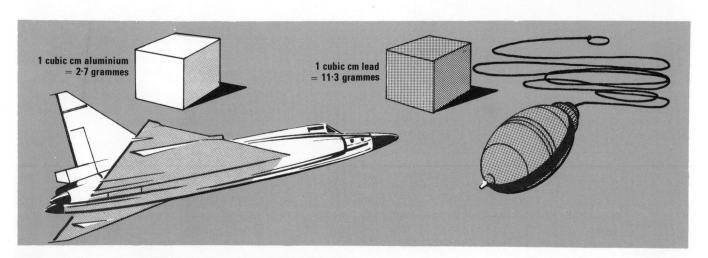

1 cubic cm aluminium = 2·7 grammes

1 cubic cm lead = 11·3 grammes

Which is the heaviest common metal?

The most common metals to be found on Earth are magnesium, aluminium, zinc, tin, iron, copper, nickel and lead. They are listed here in order of increasing density. Magnesium is the lightest and lead is the heaviest. Lead is nearly seven times as heavy as magnesium and over four times as heavy as aluminium.

Magnesium is obtained mainly from sea water in which it is found as the compound magnesium chloride. Pure magnesium is light, but not strong, so it is mainly used as an *alloy*, combined with other metals to give it strength.

Aluminium is the third most abundant element in the Earth's crust, but it is not found naturally in its pure form. It is mined and extracted from bauxite ore. Aluminium is light and strong and is used for building structures that require these properties, such as aircraft.

Lead is most commonly used in the lead plates for certain batteries where the reaction of the lead with sulphuric acid produces an electric current.

Iron is the most useful metal of our time. In fact, millions of tonnes of iron are used constantly for making steel.

How was coal formed?

About 350 million years ago there were flat swamps and forests of huge fern-like trees in many parts of the Earth. This was known as the *Carboniferous Period*.

Today, that part of the Earth's surface is buried deep underground; under the plains, under mountains, under the sea, and even under the ice of Antarctica. The climate of Antarctica has changed drastically, since that time, from a sub-tropical to a polar climate.

Other changes have taken place on the surface of the Earth, too. When the great trees died, they fell into the swamps, decomposed and were buried under the deep layers of sand and sediments carried by water. Movements in the Earth's crust caused the land to buckle and tilt. Mountains grew, shorelines changed. More forests grew up as the water went down, only to be buried themselves.

The great pressure of the weight of the sediments pressing on top of the layers of dead vegetation caused it to turn into *seams* of the hard, black rock we know as coal.

There is a wide range of types of coal, depending on how much pressure the seams have been under. *Lignite* is a young, brown form of coal. *Anthracite* is the oldest and hardest form. *Peat*, which is found at the surface on open boggy land, is also a form of coal.

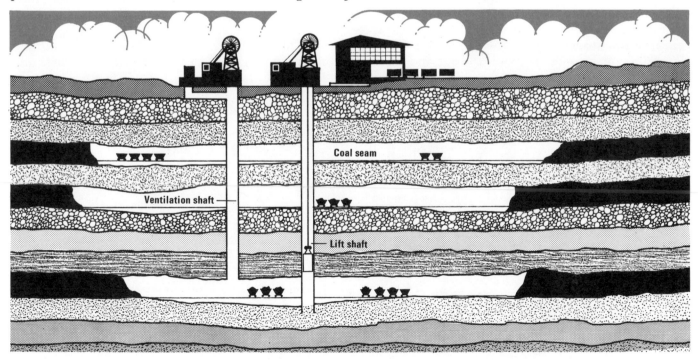

Coal seam

Ventilation shaft

Lift shaft

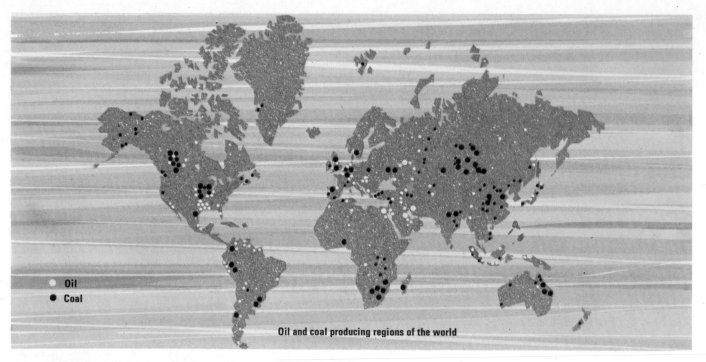

○ Oil

● Coal

Oil and coal producing regions of the world

Where does oil come from?

Oil is a dark black liquid that comes from inside the Earth. In this form it is known as crude oil or petroleum.

The name petroleum means *rock oil*, and great pools of oil are found in traps between layers of rock, which have been folded to form anticlines, or faults. It is thought that the oil may have formed from the remains of tiny plants and animals that lived in the shallow seas in prehistoric times. The remains were probably compressed, and then later turn-ed into oil. This liquid seeped into the sedimentary rocks, such as sandstone, which were formed in the shallow seas. Later, non-porous rock, which allows no liquid to seep through, formed above them, so trapping the oil beneath it.

Geologists study rock forma-tions to find probable locations of oil fields. They drill through the surface rocks, and when they eventually strike oil, it is pumped out and carried by pipeline to oil tankers, which transport it all over the world.

After the crude oil has been purified, or *refined*, it has many important uses. It provides power, through engines and machinery, and is used as fuel to generate electricity and heat. The refining process also provides the source material for many other *by-products* such as plastics, explo-sives, paints, detergents, anti-septics, cosmetics, drugs, anaes-thetics, fertilizers, weedkillers, insect sprays, synthetic fibres and nylon.

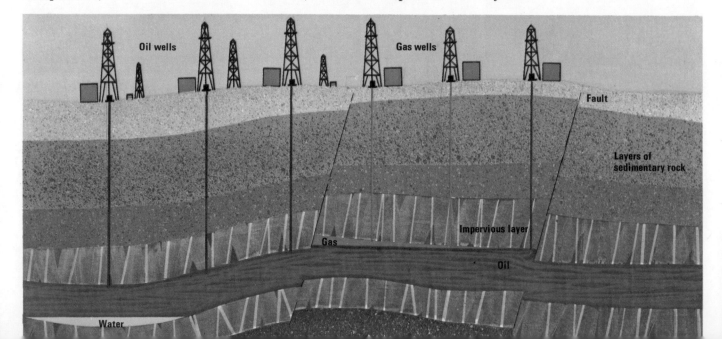

Oil wells

Gas wells

Fault

Layers of sedimentary rock

Impervious layer

Gas

Oil

Water

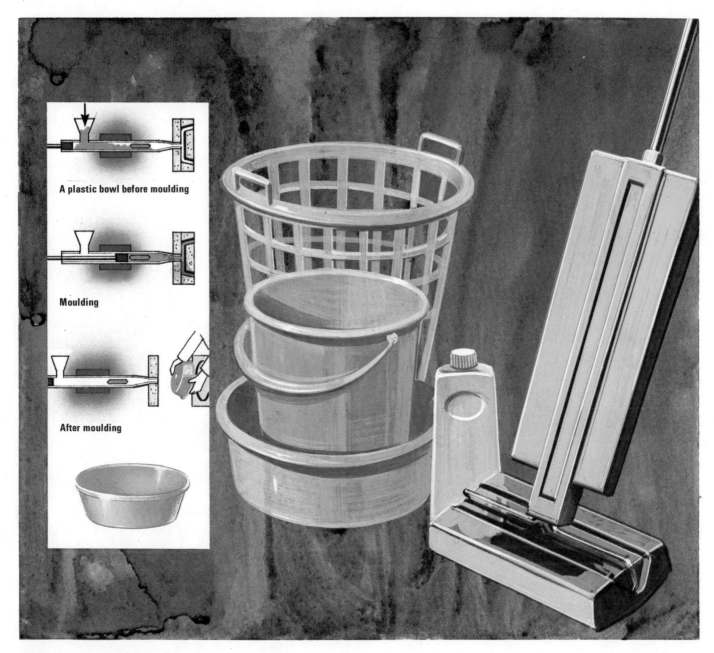

A plastic bowl before moulding

Moulding

After moulding

What are plastics?

Plastics are man-made materials. There are so many varieties that they can be moulded into any shape, made in any colour and of any strength.

Plastics are made from synthetic resins which are made up of chains of molecules. These are known as polymers. They are manufactured from coal, limestones, petroleum, salt and water.

Hard plastics, such as melamine, are used for dishes, instrument cases and hard-wearing surfaces.

Soft plastics such as polythene are used for toys, bottles and foam rubber.

Transparent plastics can be hard or soft, such as vinyl or polystyrene and are used in medicine and for packaging.

Laminated plastics, made up in layers are used decoratively. Mixed with fillers such as glass fibre, asbestos, wood or metal, they make reinforced plastics which can be very resistant to heat or corrosion.

Nylon is a type of plastic that can be used for tough work in the form of gear wheels, or woven into delicate fabric from fine fibres.

Plastic fibres such as nylon, orlon and dacron, are very light and they are also stain resistant.

The name plastic means 'able to be moulded', and plastics are shaped by many methods including moulding, casting, layering, extruding and callendering.

Why does iron go rusty?

Oil

Water

Nails are perfect

Rusty nails

Anything made of iron that is left in a damp atmosphere will begin to rust quickly unless it is protected or treated.

Rust is the film of reddish-brown powder that forms on the surface of the iron. It is formed by the iron reacting chemically with oxygen and water to form an iron oxide.

Rust can appear overnight, and if left for days, the iron will become pitted as more and more of it rusts away.

To prevent iron rusting it must be kept completely dry. This can be done by coating it with a film of oil or grease, or by plating it with another metal.

Food cans are plated with tin. Sheets of iron for building are usually coated with zinc by a process called *galvanization*.

Rusting is the name given to the behaviour of iron. When other metals become pitted by chemical reaction it is called corrosion.

What is slate?

Slate is a type of rock formed by the action of pressure on clay. It is composed of a mineral compound containing aluminium.

The clay was once the silt that formed underwater. Clay is laid down in horizontal layers. It dries and hardens to form *shale*.

Where huge Earth movements took place, the layers of shale were tipped and folded and crushed under enormous pressure and heat. They turned to slate.

Slate can be split into flat slabs. It splits at right angles to the bedding plane and streaks in the slate sometimes show this.

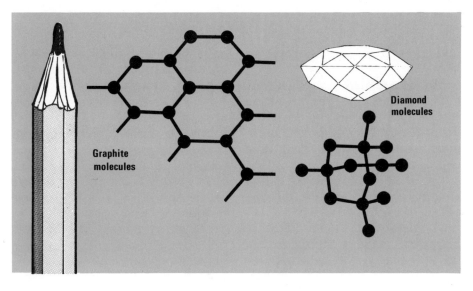

Graphite molecules

Diamond molecules

What do a pencil and a diamond have in common?

Although the blacklead in a pencil does not look at all like a diamond, they are actually made of the same chemical substance. That substance is carbon.

But the pencil contains *graphite* which is a soft, black, glossy form of carbon. Diamond is also pure carbon, but is pale and transparent. It is the hardest natural substance.

The difference is due to the crystal structure of the molecules.

What are minerals?

Minerals are substances that can be taken from the Earth. There are over two thousand kinds, but only about a hundred are common. They range from substances such as salt and the rare metals, to compounds such as bauxite which is an ore containing aluminium.

Mineralogists define minerals as the substances with the following four common properties. They are found occurring naturally. They are made from inorganic matter, that is matter that has never been part of a living organism. Each mineral has the same chemical composition, wherever it comes from. The atoms of the substance form a regular pattern, as can be seen in a crystal.

The most common mineral is quartz, which is found in most rocks. Sand on the seashore is made up mainly of the tiny, glassy fragments of quartz, which is very hard. These have been worn down by constant rubbing against other fragments, caused by movement of water.

The mineral wealth of a country includes any precious or plentiful metals and other inorganic mineral substances that can be found there. It also includes the amount of coal and oil that can be found in that country. These are of course, organic in their origin.

Are all metals shiny?

If you pick up a hard, cold, grey, evenly shaped piece of material, how can you find out what it is? Is it a bone, a stone, or a lump of wood? Or is it metal?

If you bang it and it makes a ringing sound; if you can bend it without it breaking; if it feels cold when you touch it, but it quickly warms up in your hand, then it is probably a metal. If you rub or scratch it, and it shines, then it is definitely a metal.

All the substances found on Earth are made up from basic elements. There are over a hundred different elements. Nearly three-quarters of them are metals, and all metals are lustrous, or shiny.

Metals are also sonorous; they make a ringing sound when struck. They can be cast or formed into shapes, and they are good conductors of heat and electricity.

The study of metals is called *metallurgy* and is one of the oldest branches of science.

The beautiful lustre of pure metal has made it highly valued for decorative metalwork for hundreds of years. But metals have many important practical uses. Before glass was invented, mirrors were made of shiny polished metal such as silver or bronze. Shiny metal surfaces also reflect heat as well as light.

All these properties of metals are put to good use. Because it is sonorous, bells are cast from metal. Because they are good conductors of electricity and heat, metals are used for electric cables and wires, and for cooking equipment and radiators. Because shiny metal reflects heat well, it is used for reflectors. Because metals can be shaped into such a variety of forms, making strong durable structures, they have always been immensely valuable to men.

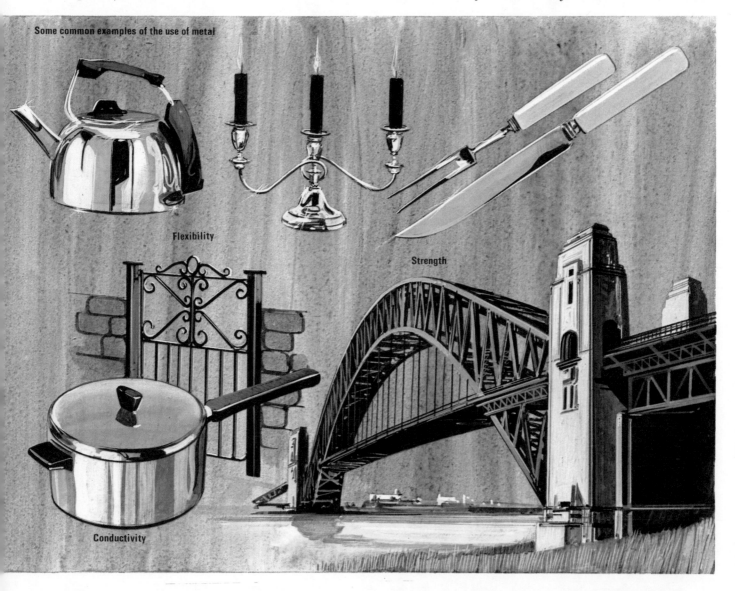

Some common examples of the use of metal

Flexibility

Strength

Conductivity

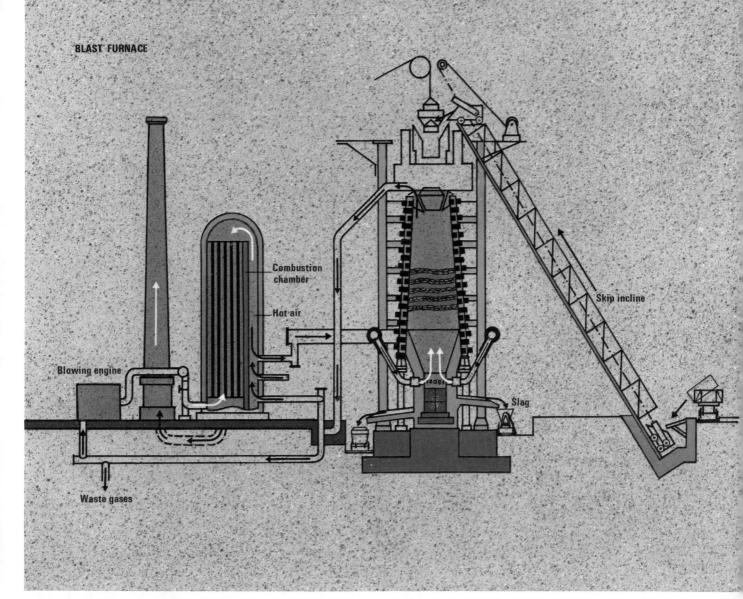

Combustion chamber

Hot air

Blowing engine

Skip incline

Slag

Waste gases

How is steel made?

Steel is iron from which most of the carbon has been removed. This is done by heating pig iron in a special, hot furnace.

The iron comes from iron ore which is mined from the earth. The ore is mixed with coke and limestone and is then heated in a blast furnace. The molten iron is run off and allowed to cool into slabs. It is then called pig iron.

Iron tends to be brittle, to corrode, and is not easily worked into many useful shapes. So pig iron is converted into steel, which has better properties.

Pig iron is heated by burning it in a stream of gas and air. Oxygen in the air combines with the ele-

ment *carbon* in the molten iron. They form the gas *carbon dioxide*. The metal which remains contains less than two percent of carbon.

By adding certain amounts of other elements to the melt, various types of steel are produced. Some are particularly hard, others very good for drawing into wires and so on. Another property that can be influenced is the *conductivity*. This is the ability to pass heat, or electricity along something. Steel is a good heat conductor.

It is because of this fast rate of heat conduction that metals feel hot in hot weather and cold in

cold. When you touch something metal that has been out in the Sun, it will feel hotter than your hand because it has absorbed more heat from the Sun than your body. But if you touch something metal on a cold day, it feels particularly cold. It has lost its heat more quickly than your body.

Steel is one of the most important materials of our time and we are sometimes compared with our ancestors by being described as living in the steel age.

The first industrial method for producing steel was invented in 1856 by Henry Bessemer (1813–1898). His method was known as the Bessemer process.

How big is an atom?

Atoms are the building blocks of all matter. They are so minute that a very small lump of the metal copper, weighing only a gram and being smaller than a sugar lump, would contain nearly ten thousand million million million atoms.

The countless number of different substances on Earth are made up from just over one hundred basic substances, called *elements*. These can combine or react with each other to form new substances. The smallest part of an element that can take part in a reaction, is called an atom.

For many years, men thought that atoms were solid and indestructible. Then it was discovered that the body of an atom is concentrated at its centre, called the nucleus. The nucleus is made up of two types of particles, *protons* and *neutrons*. The atom behaves as if it were ten thousand times bigger than just the nucleus because tiny particles, called *electrons*, whirl round the nucleus like planets round the Sun. But they move so fast that they seem to form a solid, outer shell.

Atoms combine or share their electrons with those of other atoms. This is how atoms of different elements combine to form *compound* substances.

Right: An enlarged atom as it might appear if it could be slowed down. Electrons might be seen travelling round the nucleus.

Right: An atom as it might appear if greatly enlarged.

What is a molecule?

A molecule is the smallest portion of a substance that can exist on its own. A molecule of the gas hydrogen contains one atom of the element hydrogen. A molecule of the gas oxygen contains two atoms of the element oxygen. A molecule of water contains one atom of hydrogen and two atoms of oxygen. The molecules of hydrogen and oxygen have combined to form the compound water. Water is the most common compound on the Earth.

There are millions of different compounds. A great many of them contain the element carbon and these are called organic compounds.

The way the molecules are arranged in a substance affects its behaviour. In a solid, the molecules have a regular arrangement called its crystal structure. In a liquid the molecules are free to move about, although they are still attracted to each other, so a liquid flows. In a gas, the molecules are free to move about in any direction. They also vibrate very fast. So a gas tends to expand to fill its container.

Solids change to liquids because molecules have begun to break away from their positions in the crystal structure. This occurs when the substance is heated so that the molecules vibrate faster. If the liquid is heated, the molecules vibrate faster still, until some of them break out of the surface. The liquid is then boiling.

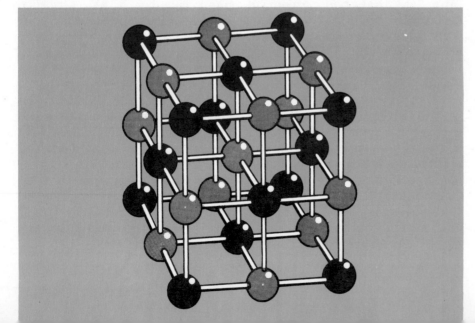

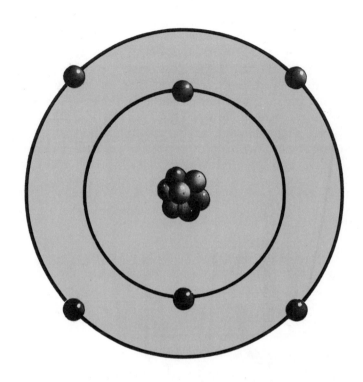

Right: An enlarged atom as it might appear if halted completely. It looks like our solar system. Protons and neutrons are in the centre (the 'sun') and electrons are seen around it (the 'planets').

What are elements?

The elements are the 103 different substances that make up all the matter on Earth. All the atoms in an element are alike. This means that an element cannot be broken down into more simple substances.

There are two kinds of elements; these are metals and non-metals. The most common metals include magnesium, aluminium, zinc, tin, iron, copper, nickel and lead.

There are only 92 different elements which occur naturally, the last one being uranium. All the others are obtained from nuclear reactions.

Some elements exist in more than one form. The different forms are known as *isotopes*. Different isotopes of an element have a different number of neutrons in the nucleus of an atom.

ELEMENTS

		Wt				Wt
⊙	Hydrogen	1	⊕	Strontian	46
⊘	Azote	5	✳	Barytes	68
●	Carbon	5,4	Ⓘ	Iron	50
○	Oxygen	7	Ⓩ	Zinc	56
⊗	Phosphorus	9	Ⓒ	Copper	56
⊕	Sulphur	13	Ⓛ	Lead	90
⟳	Magnesia	20	Ⓢ	Silver	190
⊖	Lime	24	Ⓖ	Gold	190
⊜	Soda	28	Ⓟ	Plantina	190
⊜	Potash	42	✻	Mercury	161

Left: In 1808–1810 John Dalton, the founder of modern atomic theory, drew up this table of elements. It shows their symbols and their atomic weights.

What happens in a chemical reaction?

In a chemical reaction, substances react together to form one or more new substances. The appearance of the new substance may be quite different from those from which it is made. Copper, which is a bright, reddish metal reacts with the colourless gas oxygen. Together they form the substance copper oxide, which is a pale green colour. You may have noticed some of it on old copper coins. Shiny silver turns yellow and then black as it reacts with oxygen to form silver oxide.

In both these reactions, some of the metal atoms have joined with oxygen molecules to form oxide molecules.

A chemical reaction can bring about a change of state.

There are three important types of compound that are involved in many reactions. They are called acids, alkalis (or bases) and salts. When an acid is mixed with an alkali the two always react to produce a salt and also water. For example, hydrogen chloride is the acid found in our stomachs. When hydrochloric acid is mixed with the strong alkali, sodium hydroxide, or washing soda, the products of the reaction are water and sodium chloride, better known as common salt.

Below: A chemical reaction can be seen in this picture. Sodium, which is a grey metallic element, has been put together with chloride, a poisonous gas. Together they have produced sodium chloride (salt).

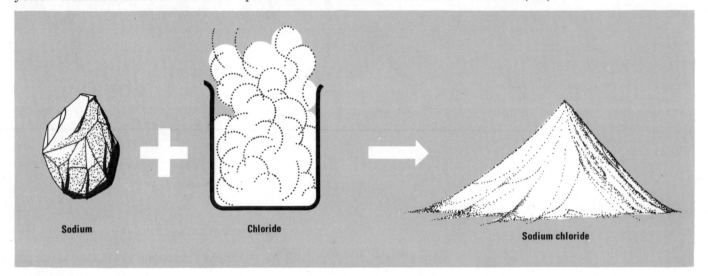

Sodium   Chloride   Sodium chloride

What is acid?

An acid is a sour, corrosive liquid that turns litmus solution red. (Litmus is made from a lichen plant. It has a special use in chemistry as an *indicator*. It indicates that acid is present.)

Acids corrode metals by 'eating' them away. A molecule of acid consists of one or more hydrogen atoms combined with one or more other atoms. When an acid reacts with a metal, the hydrogen is freed and the other atoms in the acid combine with the metal to form a *salt*.

Some of the common acids are hydrochloric acid, sulphuric acid and nitric acid.

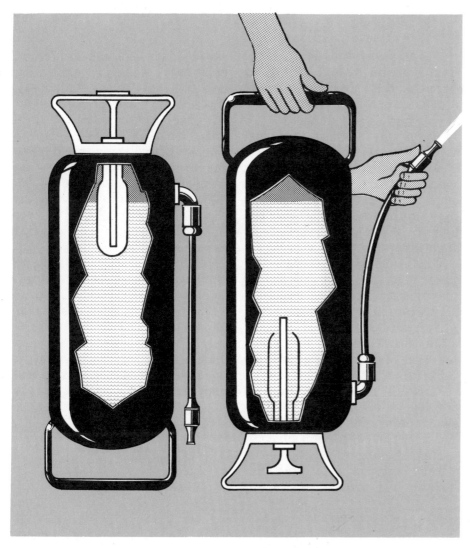

How does a fire extinguisher work?

One common type is the carbon dioxide extinguisher, which can be quite small and held in the hand. By squeezing the trigger, a jet of solid carbon dioxide, which is like snow, is expelled. This changes to carbon dioxide gas, which is a heavy gas that does not 'support combustion'. That is, it falls, like a blanket, over the fire, keeping out the air and oxygen that would keep the fire burning. It can be used on most types of fire, including electrical fires.

Foam fire extinguishers cannot be used on electrical fires. They are used mainly on fires involving burning oil or petrol. The foam is produced by the chemical reaction of aluminium sulphate with sodium bicarbonate and water. The two chemicals are stored separately and are mixed when the metal container is turned upside down.

Soda-acid extinguishers are also one of the most common types. The metal container holds a solution of sodium carbonate in water and a small bottle of sulphuric acid. When the extinguisher is turned upside down, a plunger opens the acid bottle so that all the contents of the container mix together. The chemical reaction produces carbon dioxide gas, which builds up the pressure inside the container. The pressure causes a powerful jet of water to shoot out which can be directed onto the fire. This type cannot be used on electrical fires either, because some of the chemicals remain dissolved in the water. This makes the water conductive. The person holding the extinguisher might receive a fatal shock if an electric current passed back to him along the water jet.

Carbon tetrachloride extinguishers can be used on electrical fires. In these, the jet is produced by compressed air.

Why do you put bicarbonate on a bee sting?

When a bee stings you, it injects you with acid. To stop the sting hurting the acid must be neutralized, by adding alkali. The most convenient alkaline compound likely to be found in the home is bicarbonate-of-soda which is used in baking powder.

Animals use their stings to protect themselves. Some plants use a similar *defence mechanism*. Nettles sting by pricking your skin with the tiny hairs on their leaves. This releases drops of *histamine*.

How are photographs made?

Light makes the compound silver bromide turn black. Photographic film, which is made of transparent plastic film, is coated with an emulsion of silver bromide mixed with gelatin.

In the camera, one part of the roll of film is exposed to the light by opening the *shutter* for a fraction of a second. The *lens* behind the shutter focuses the light onto the film, producing a small, sharp image of the scene or object in front of the shutter. The bright, light parts of the object reflect the most light. Where this reflected light falls on the film, the silver bromide turns darkest. The shades vary in proportion to the amount of light reflected from different areas. Where the object is dark or black, no light is reflected and the bromide is unaffected.

Another photograph is taken by winding the film on until the next unexposed part of the film is in front of the shutter.

The exposed film is removed from the camera and kept away from the light. Films are usually processed in a *dark room*.

The film is developed with a solution that turns the most exposed parts of the silver bromide to a black form of silver. On the partly exposed areas, not so many crystals are affected so these are more transparent. The unexposed areas will appear as clear film.

This is called the *negative* because it is the exact opposite of the object that was photographed: dark where it was light and light where it was dark.

The situation now has to be reversed to obtain a picture like the original subject.

First the negative is *fixed* in another solution that washes away the unused silver bromide and fixes the crystals in place.

Then the negative is placed in a frame against a piece of light-sensitive photographic paper.

This is then exposed to a short, calculated flash of light. The negative lets most light pass through its clear parts, causing the photographic emulsion to be most exposed at these points. These parts will come out dark on the developed print, just as they were in the original scene. The dark parts of the negative let through the least light, or even none. So these parts appear white or very pale on the photograph, just as they were originally. All the correct shades of brightness in between are reproduced, too.

The photographic paper has to be developed and fixed in the same way as the negative. This produces a complete black and white image of the subject that was photographed.

Below: The different stages involved in making photographs. We can see how black and white films are developed and how prints are made from negatives.

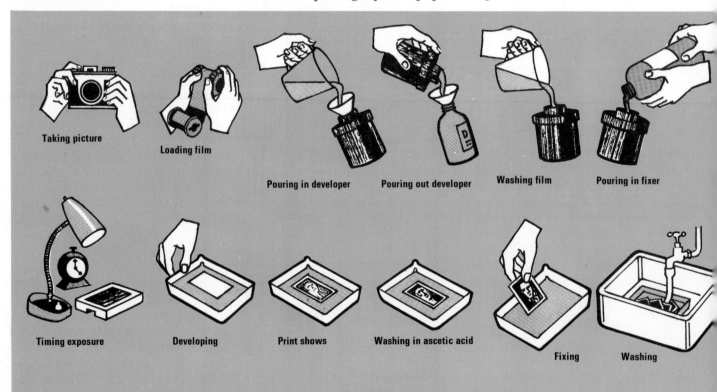

Taking picture

Loading film

Pouring in developer

Pouring out developer

Washing film

Pouring in fixer

Timing exposure

Developing

Print shows

Washing in ascetic acid

Fixing

Washing

How is glass made?

The ancient Egyptians knew how to make glass. The art was lost for thousands of years but now we are used to seeing it everywhere. Its most useful property is that it is transparent: it allows light to pass through it. So for centuries it has been used for windows.

Glass is made from sand, soda and limestone. These are heated together at a high temperature. They melt to form a liquid that hardens into clear, smooth glass. To make it completely transparent, the surface has to be ground and polished.

Glass can be moulded into many useful shapes. It can be poured into moulds and allowed to set, or it can be blown into hollow shapes.

Glass-blowing is a highly skilled craft. Many beautiful designs have been produced. Most useful articles are machine-moulded but cut-glass is still popular. Other techniques for making decorative glass involve etching, twisting and staining the glass with colours.

Plate glass is produced rather like sheet metal, by passing it between rollers. A more recent development is float glass. In this process huge sheets of perfectly flat glass are produced by floating the molten mixture on molten tin, which has a higher melting point than glass.

There are many different types of glass available. Ordinary glass is brittle, toughened glass is far stronger. A special type is used for car windscreens. It does not shatter into pieces, but merely cracks evenly all over. A zoned windscreen leaves a patch for the driver to see through. Pyrex is heat resistant and so is used for laboratory and cooking equipment. Glass fibre is a jumble of fine glass threads and is a good insulator. Mixed with a plastic it also makes very strong, durable material and car bodies, caravans, boat hulls and furniture are some of its uses.

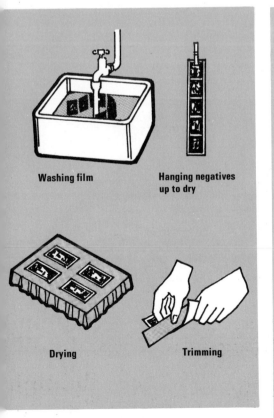

Washing film

Hanging negatives up to dry

Drying

Trimming

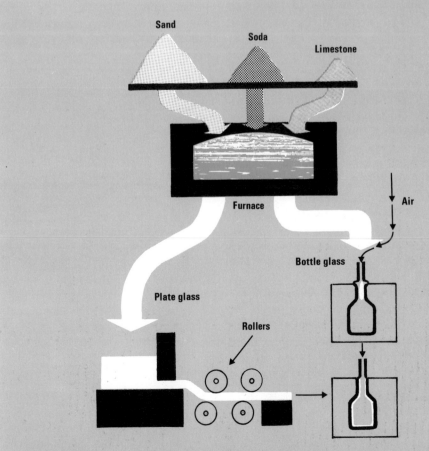

Sand

Soda

Limestone

Furnace

Air

Bottle glass

Plate glass

Rollers

What is power?

Power is the rate at which work is done. It used to be measured in *horsepower*. One horsepower was the amount of power used when a horse, or anything, raised a weight of 550 pounds through one foot in one second. Now we measure power in units called *watts*.

In electrical terms, a watt is the energy used up by an electric current of one amp when it flows through a conductor across a potential difference of one volt.

The *kilowatt* is a more useful unit than the watt. 1 kilowatt = 1000 watts. An electric fire might use about two kilowatts, whereas an electric light bulb might use only 100 watts.

How does a petrol combustion engine work?

In a petrol combustion engine, a combustible vapour (one that can be set on fire) is exploded inside a closed *cylinder*. The force of the explosion provides the power to drive a moveable *piston* out of the cylinder.

First the piston travels to the top of the cylinder and a valve opens to allow a mixture of air and petrol into the cylinder. The petrol vapourizes and the mixture is highly inflammable. The valve then closes to allow the process to be completed.

The mixture is ignited, or set on fire, by a *sparking plug*, which is also in the top of the cylinder. The spark is produced by an electric current jumping across the gap between the *points* of the plug.

The vapour explodes and expands rapidly. To make room for the expanded, burning gas, the piston is forced to move down the cylinder in which it slides. (If the piston does not fit well, the cylinder loses *compression*.)

A second valve opens to allow the exhaust gases to escape. They are driven out by the rising piston.

The piston starts to descend, and the cycle begins again. The first valve then opens once more to let in more petrol for vapourizing.

Most ordinary cars have four-cylinder engines, with each cylinder sparking in turn. More powerful cars have more cylinders.

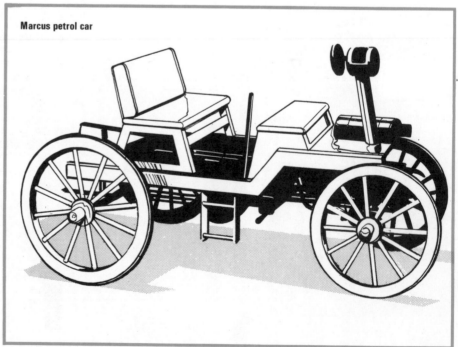

Marcus petrol car

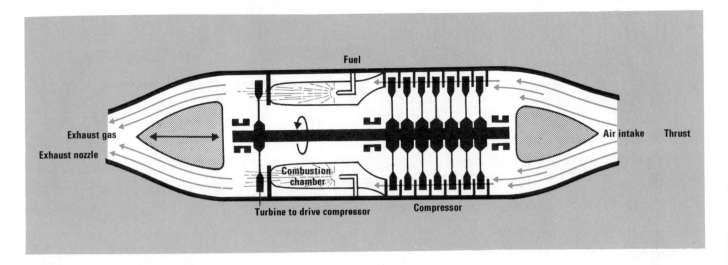

What is a turbo-jet?

If you blow up a balloon and let it go, it will fly across the room by *jet propulsion*. The jet of air escaping quickly from the hole at the back produces a thrusting force at the front. It is this thrusting which makes the balloon shoot forwards.

Jet-propelled aircraft fly through the air. They are forced along by streams of hot gas which are emitted from their *gas-turbine* engines.

The engine draws in air at the front. The air is compressed and then passes into the *combustion chamber*, where it is used to burn the fuel. This produces an extremely powerful jet of hot gas which escapes through the exhaust at the back, thrusting the plane forward.

The hot gas rushing out also turns the blades of a turbine, like a windmill. The turbine drives the compressor which compresses the air.

Jet engines have enabled aircraft to be designed which can fly at twice the speed of sound. Such high speeds would never have been possible with propellor driven aircraft.

How does a plane fly?

An aeroplane is made to fly by means of the forward thrust, produced by its propellors or jets. It is kept up in the air by the resulting lifting force on its wings.

The first flights were made in balloons that rose upwards when filled with hot air from a fire lit beneath the balloon. The next success with flight came with gliders, which fly like birds once they are in the air. Their tilted wings create a slight upward lift, keeping them up as they glide forward.

The first successful powered flights were made by the Wright brothers in 1903. It was the invention of the internal combustion engine that made powered flight possible. This was the only engine

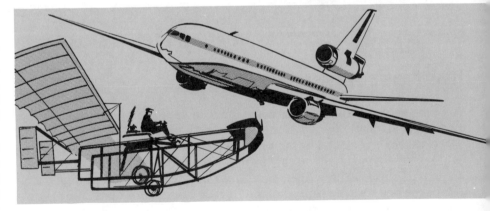

using light enough fuel that could produce enough forward thrust and hence lifting power, for the machine to fly. The Wright brothers' plane had a petrol engine.

The lifting effect is produced by the shape of the wings. The under surface is shorter in length than the longer curved upper surface. Air flowing over the

Above: Two examples of early and modern aircraft. On the left is one of the tail-first monoplanes of 1911 and on the right is the McDonnell Douglas DC-10 of the 1970s.

wings as the plane is thrust forward, experiences an increase in pressure on the underside of the wing and a reduction in pressure on the top side. This difference in pressure creates the lifting force.

39

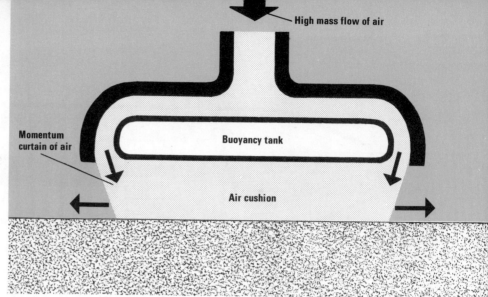

High mass flow of air

Momentum curtain of air

Buoyancy tank

Air cushion

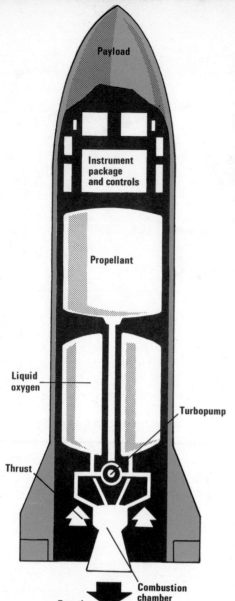

Payload

Instrument package and controls

Propellant

Liquid oxygen

Turbopump

Thrust

Combustion chamber

Reaction

What keeps a hovercraft afloat?

The hovercraft is an *amphibious* vehicle. It can travel on land or in water. (An *amphibian* is an animal, such as a frog, that can live on land or in water.)

The hovercraft can travel over any type of surface because it moves on top of its own cushion of air. This is produced by a large propellor or fan which blows air downwards so hard that it lifts the machine off the ground. The air escapes from under a stiff, rubber *skirt* which surrounds the edge of the base.

The air-cushion only supports the craft. It is driven forward by aircraft propellors and it is steered by rudders on the fins at the rear.

The hovercraft can move over any flat surface, but it does not need to be smooth. It has been ideal as transport in water, rough country, on building sites and over undulating ground. Some of the great rivers of Africa and South America have been explored by means of a hovercraft.

How does a space rocket fly?

A space rocket cannot fly like an ordinary aircraft, because there is no air in outer space for propellors to drive it through, nor to provide lift on the wings.

Space rockets are jet-propelled. Fuel is burnt in a combustion chamber. It produces hot gases which escape through the nozzle forcing the rocket forwards.

Unlike jet aircraft engines, the space rocket does not draw in any air from the front, or from anywhere outside. There is no air in outer space. Instead of air, the fuel has to be mixed with an *oxidant*, to make the fuel burn. It is usually liquid oxygen. The fuel

is known as the *propellant*.

In the Saturn V rocket, which was used to launch the Apollo spacecraft on their Moon missions, there are three stages. The first stage uses paraffin (kerosene) as the propellant, while the second and third stages use liquid hydrogen.

The Earth's gravitational force tends to pull everything down towards it. Rockets have to reach a speed called the *escape velocity*, to escape from the Earth's pull. This is a velocity of 11·2 kilometres per second.

Once it is out in space, side jets provide the rocket with sideways

thrust so that it can be steered on a course.

It will continue to fly onwards until it comes within the gravitational field of another body, such as the Moon or another planet.

For a rocket to travel to a distant planet, and for it to return, would require more fuel than any rocket can yet carry. The load a rocket carries is called the *payload*. This must not be too great at lift off if the rocket is to leave the ground. Scientists are developing nuclear-powered rockets that carry a small reactor aboard. This generates nuclear power to drive the rocket's engines.

How does a ship sail?

There are similarities between a ship's sails and an aircraft's wings, in that they are both curved in shape so that air flowing past creates a lifting force. A ship's sails are specially shaped so that they are not just flat sheets of fabric, but slightly belled or bagged. To get the ship to sail, the sails are held in position, or *set*, so that the wind blows across one side of the bows and fills out the sail. Wind flowing over the other side of the sail is at a reduced pressure, producing a driving force roughly in the direction of the bows. At the same time, the reaction of the wind deflected off the sail produces a forward reaction.

The ship is kept moving forward, instead of moving across the wind, by the reaction of the keel underneath the hull. This is held vertically in the stem to stern direction and makes the hull resist sideways movement. The rudder, which is positioned in the water astern of (behind) the keel, is used to steer the boat.

There are three basic sailing directions; sailing into the wind, with the wind blowing to within 45 degrees of the direction head-on to the ship, which involves sailing a zig-zag course, known as *tacking*; sailing across the wind; and sailing, or *running*, before the wind.

What is a calorie?

A calorie is the name of a scientific unit used as a measure of heat. One calorie is the amount of heat you would need to make the temperature of one gram of water rise 1°C.

In the international system (SI) of units, heat is measured in *joules*. One calorie equals 4·1868 joules, in SI units.

The calorie is used to describe the amount of heat that can be provided by fuels. Food is a fuel. We burn it up as energy; it is converted to mechanical energy by our muscles. The energy value of foods is sometimes quoted in calories. People who are trying to lose weight eat a carefully controlled low calorie diet so that they do not store surplus fuel as fat on their bodies.

It is important to notice that the unit of heat is the calorie (with a small c) and the unit used for food values is the Calorie (with a capital C). The Calorie is also known as the kilogram-calorie which equals 1000 calories.

What is energy?

In the world of physics, the term energy has an exact meaning. It is a body's capacity to do work. Energy cannot be created, nor can it be destroyed. This is one of the physical laws that governs our universe. Energy is constantly being converted from one form to another.

Potential energy is the energy a body has because of its position. An object high off the ground, or up a hill, will fall down because of the pull of gravity on it. The body will do work to reach its position of zero potential energy at ground level.

It will then possess *kinetic energy*, the energy of a body due to its movement. If friction brings the body to a halt, the kinetic energy may be changed to heat. Kinetic energy can be harnessed to produce electrical energy.

Electrical energy is the result of the movement of parts of atoms, called electrons. Chemical energy is also stored within atoms and is released during a chemical reaction.

All matter is made up of atoms. The only form of energy that can exist in the absence of atoms is radiant energy. We obtain energy from the Sun as radiant energy.

People, especially children, are described as being very energetic, or having a lot of energy, if they are very strong, active and enthu-

Where does energy come from?

Energy comes to the Earth from the Sun in the form of *electromagnetic radiation*. We see it as heat and light. Plants use it to grow, starting the food chain which eventually provides humans with muscular energy. Most of the fuels, such as coal, oil and gas, which we use to power our machines, were originally living matter. Water power involves the Sun's energy too; the hot Sun makes the water evaporate. The clouds of water vapour are blown inland and fall as rain on high ground. This is an enormous source of potential energy as all the water has to run downhill to the sea again.

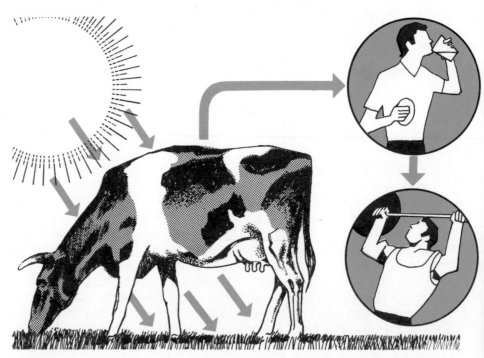

siastic. They probably have extra, or *surplus*, energy because they are healthy, fit and well fed. Their muscles are strong and their bodies burn up the food they eat.

Above: A lot of our energy comes from the Sun. Plants need the Sun to grow, and they are eaten by animals. The animals in turn provide us with food.

Why do things fall?

Objects fall to the ground because of the force, known as *gravity*. If you drop an apple, you see the effect of the force of the Earth's gravity pulling it towards the centre of the Earth. In fact, the Earth is also attracted to the apple at the same time, but its movement is negligible. Everything solid has a gravitational force. The strength of an object's gravitational force depends on its mass. The gravity on the Moon is only about one sixth of that on Earth.

The Sun has a very strong gravitational pull which holds the planets in their orbits. This is what keeps the Earth moving round the Sun, and prevents it from flying off into space.

If you drop an apple and a piece of paper at the same time, from the same height, the apple will reach the ground before the piece of paper. Gravity seems to pull the apple faster than the paper, but this is not so. The force of gravity makes all bodies accelerate towards the Earth at the same rate. It is air resistance that slows down the piece of paper. If the experiment is repeated with a small apple and a large one, they will both land at the same time.

The laws of gravity were studied and set out by the famous English scientist, Sir Isaac Newton.

What is weightlessness?

When you pick up an object, you can feel whether it is heavy or light. You feel its *weight*, that is, the effect of the Earth's gravity on it. We have seen how all objects are pulled towards the Earth by the gravitational force. That is, how they stay on its surface without being spun off into space.

The weight of an object depends on its mass, that is, the amount of matter it contains, and also on its position on the Earth. The higher above the Earth it is, the lighter its weight. An object weighs less at the top of a high mountain than it does at sea level.

The effect of the Earth's gravity is reduced the further away from the Earth's surface it moves. Anything in a spaceship grows lighter as it travels away from the Earth. It is said to be weightless.

Astronauts have to learn to adapt to weightlessness. They are able to float about in the spacecraft cabin. Their equipment would float about too, if it were not fastened down.

Why do passengers fall over when a bus starts?

An object does not usually start to move by itself. For example, a football will not move unless it is kicked. To start something moving, a force has to be applied to it. In the case of the football, the force is applied by the kick.

This tendency of things to stay in the same place unless motivated by an external force, is called *inertia*.

Passengers standing in a bus or train show this tendency. When the bus starts, they tend to fall backwards, because their bodies were stationary and wanted to stay like that.

Objects that are moving at a constant speed tend to continue moving, even when a force is applied to stop them. When the bus stops suddenly, all the people lurch forwards.

What is perpetual motion?

This is really a trick question. A perpetual motion machine would have to make its own energy. This is impossible because energy cannot be created, or destroyed. This is one of the main laws of physics.

The whole purpose of a machine is to convert one form of energy into another form which is more useful. For example, an electric kettle converts electrical energy into heat, which is another form of energy.

When man started to make machines, he realized that all machines needed some kind of energy to make them work. Some inventors tried to think of a machine which, once started, would go on working for ever. They called the idea perpetual motion. However, no one has ever succeeded.

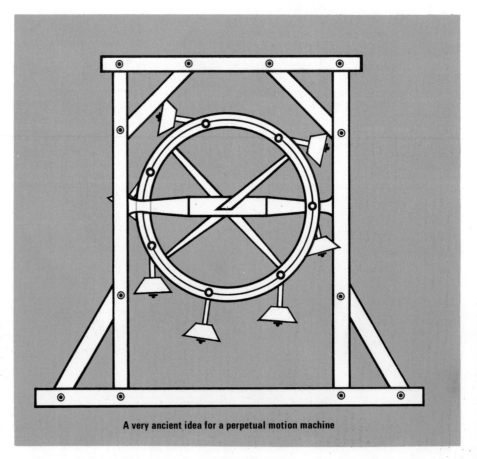

A very ancient idea for a perpetual motion machine

Why doesn't water fall out of a swinging bucket?

If you take a bucket, half full of water, and swing it round in a circle over your head, the water will not spill out, if you swing it quickly enough.

If you simply turn the bucket upside down, the water will just pour out. Water always falls towards the Earth because of the force of gravity. This force is the pull the Earth exerts on the water.

But when an object moves in a circle, another force acts on it, the centrifugal force. This acts outwards from the centre of the circle along the radius. The centrifugal force increases, the faster the object travels.

When the bucket of water is swung round in a circle quickly, the water will stay in the bucket if the centrifugal force is greater than the force of gravity.

How does a spin drier dry?

A spin drier is really quite a simple machine. It makes use of the basic principle of centrifugal force.

Wet clothes are put into the inner drum of the machine. Driven by an electric motor, this drum rotates at a very high speed. Centrifugal force makes everything accelerate away from the centre of the drum.

The clothes are flattened against the sides and the water in them is able to escape through small holes in the perforated wall of the drum as it rotates. It falls into the stationary outer case and is drained off.

Centrifuge machines, rather like a spin drier, are used in laboratories. They can be used to drive bubbles of gas out of a liquid, and to separate liquids of different densities.

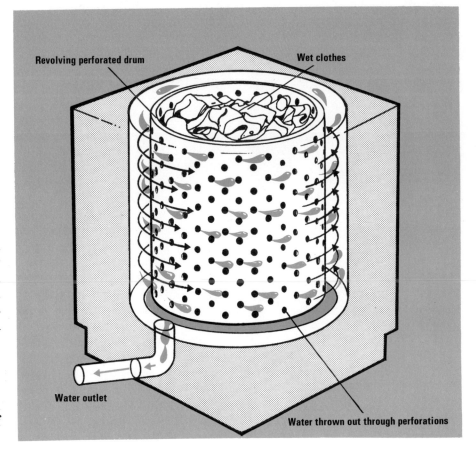

Revolving perforated drum

Wet clothes

Water outlet

Water thrown out through perforations

How is distance measured?

When measurements are being made, it is important to use the most suitable units, so the result is useful and accurate.

For example, if you want to measure how much you have grown in the last year, you should measure your height in metres and centimetres, or feet and inches. When astronomers are measuring the distance of the stars, no units we use on Earth are any use. The distance of the stars is measured in light-years (*see page* 73), that is the distance light travels in one year, which is about 300 million metres per second.

For a long time in Britain and the U.S.A., the units of length have been miles, yards, feet and inches. In Europe the metric system is used; kilometres, metres, centimetres and millimetres. This system is now being accepted internationally. It is also used for scientific work.

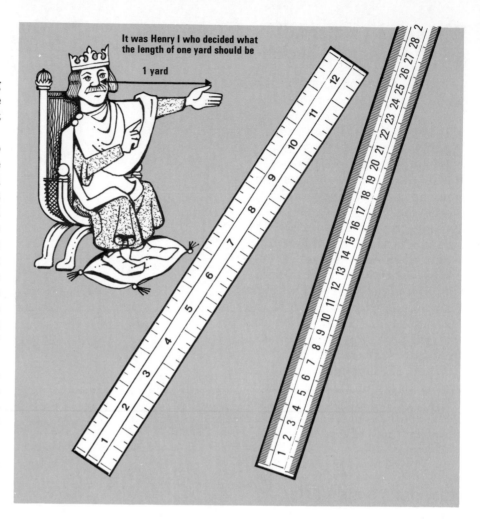

It was Henry I who decided what the length of one yard should be

1 yard

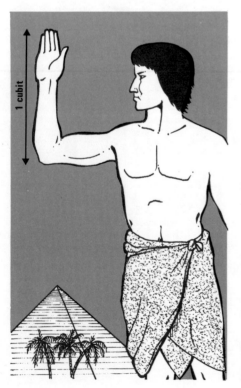

1 cubit

How long is a cubit?

A cubit is an ancient term that was used as a measurement of length. It was used by the Egyptians and is mentioned in their records describing the building of the pyramids.

A cubit is about 53 centimetres long. It was based on the distance from a man's elbow to the tip of his middle finger.

Many units have an interesting story. The knot, used in measuring speed at sea, originated from the practice of paying out a knotted rope while sailing, and counting the rate at which the evenly spaced knots were used.

The height of a horse is measured in hands. One hand is about 10 centimetres high, being the average width of a man's hand.

What is a gyroscope?

A gyroscope is a spinning wheel. It is mounted in a moveable frame in such a way that it is free to rotate about any axis. This type of mounting is known as a *universal mounting*.

The spinning axle of a gyroscope always remains pointing in the same direction. This is known as gyroscopic inertia.

Gyroscopes are used in the mountings of navigation instruments for ships, aircraft and missiles. Because of their inertia, they are not affected by the movements of the vehicle. Gyrostabilizers, incorporating gyroscopic mountings, reduce the roll of a ship at sea. Gyroscopes are used in surveying, mining and drilling equipment, too.

What is precession?

Apart from gyroscopic inertia, gyroscopes have yet another very important property. This is known as precession.

Precession is the tendency of a spinning gyroscope to move at right angles to the direction of any force applied to it, instead of in the direction of the force.

This can be seen in a bowling hoop, or a moving bicycle. If the hoop is pushed on one side, or if the cyclist leans to one side, both the hoop and bicycle keep moving. They will also change direction, turning through a right angle.

A bicycle is a good example of gyroscopic behaviour. It stays upright when the wheels are spinning because of gyroscopic inertia. You can feel the force of this inertia if you hold the front wheel of a bicycle off the ground and spin it. It is much more difficult to turn the wheel by means of the handlebars, than when the wheel is stationary.

Right: If you spin a top like this, you will see that the head of the handle also moves, while the top is spinning. While the Earth rotates round the Sun, it is also spinning on its own axis. These two principles are examples of precession.

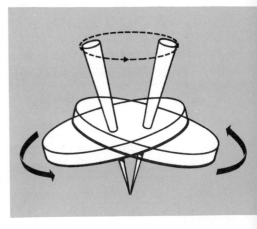

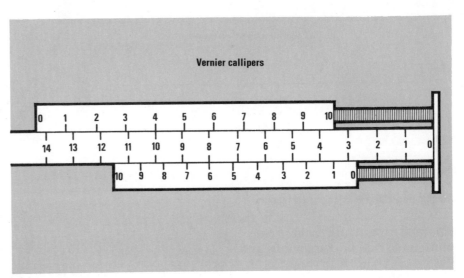

Vernier callipers

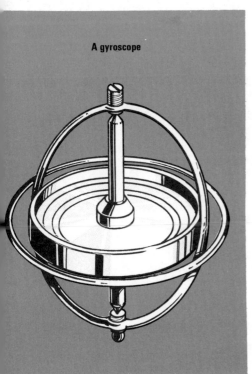

A gyroscope

What are vernier callipers?

Vernier callipers are an accurate measuring instrument used for the precise measurement of the dimensions of small objects. They take their name from Vernier, the inventor of the vernier scale. This is an attachment found on many scientific linear measuring instruments.

The callipers have jaws with parallel faces. When the jaws are closed, the pointer on the scale reads zero. The zero of the vernier scale will also be aligned with zero on the main scale, which is divided into main divisions. The main divisions are divided yet again into subdivisions of ten equal parts. The vernier scale will be of a length equal to nine of these subdivisions, and it will be divided into ten equal parts.

To read a measurement with the callipers, open the jaws and grip them lightly across the object to be measured. To read the scale, the first figure will be the number of whole main divisions left of the vernier scale zero. The next figure will be the number of whole subdivisions to the left of the vernier scale zero. The last figure is the number of that division on the vernier scale that lies directly opposite a subdivision mark on the main scale.

Callipers usually have two sets of jaws, one for making external measurements and one for making internal measurements.

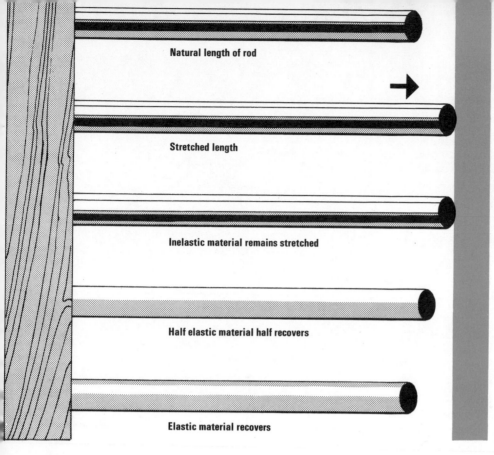

Natural length of rod

Stretched length

Inelastic material remains stretched

Half elastic material half recovers

Elastic material recovers

What is elasticity?

Most materials change their shape when put under a force that compresses or stretches them. Some do so more than others; they are said to be less *rigid*. When the pressure is removed, the changed or, deformed, object sometimes regains its original shape, depending on how much it has been deformed, and on what material it is made from.

Materials that regain their shape are *elastic*. Rubber is a well-known example. Materials, such as clay, that do not go back to their original shape at all, are inelastic.

Springs are made from elastic materials. They are designed to absorb the force of a shock and then to restore the system to its original shape and position.

Why does rubber bounce?

There are many different types of man-made rubber compounds and many of them will bounce because rubber is a highly elastic material.

When a rubber ball bounces, the rounded surface that hits the floor is flattened by the force of the impact. But because rubber is so elastic, the ball quickly starts to regain its shape and pushes itself up off the floor.

The ball never quite rises to the height it was dropped from after a bounce, because at each bounce it loses a little energy.

A round stone dropped from the same height might bounce once or twice. But it would stop sooner because it is less elastic than a rubber ball and loses more energy on each bounce.

The harder it hits the floor, the higher the ball, or stone, will bounce. The harder the floor, the more the ball will be deformed and the higher it will bounce.

How do you measure acceleration?

Acceleration is the rate at which the speed, or velocity, of a moving object increases.

Velocity is expressed in metres per second, or miles per hour, for example. This is the distance travelled, divided by the time it has taken to travel that distance.

Acceleration can be expressed in metres per second. This is the increase in velocity divided by the time taken to reach the new velocity.

In the box on the left in the picture above, the lines on the road are 15 metres apart. The velocity of the car does not change; it is travelling at a constant 15 metres per second. In the box on the right, the car is moving faster and faster. This is acceleration.

Below: This picture illustrates how the speed of animals varies greatly. A snail only moves at about 1 millimetre per second, while the cheetah, the fastest animal, can move at 26 metres per second.

Which is the fastest animal?

The animal that can move the fastest under its own power, of course, is the cheetah. It can move at over 60 miles per hour, that is about 26 metres per second.

Man's record running speed is so far only 11·8 metres per second, which is nearly 48 kilometres per hour. However, not many people can run even half as fast as this because they have never practised running. The average walking pace is less than 5 kilometres per hour.

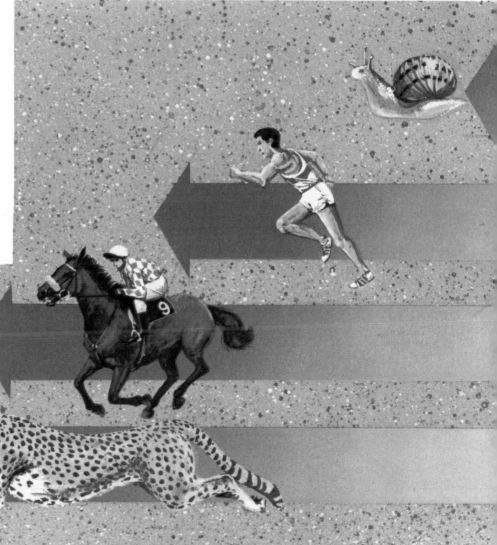

What is a leaf spring?

Leaf springs are used on vehicles to suspend the body on the axles. This prevents the passengers from being violently jolted by every bump in the road.

The springs are easy to see on old carts. They are made of layers, or leaves, of springy, steel strips. These are riveted together to make a curved metal spring that can stretch more on its outer surface than on the inner surface because it is not a solid piece of metal.

There are many other types of springs used in the suspension systems of modern vehicles.

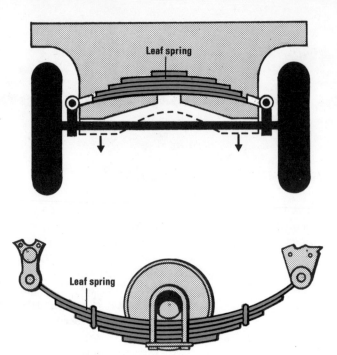

What is a fulcrum?

In any system of levers, the forces acting in it tend to produce a turning or rotating effect about one point. This point is called the fulcrum. The turning effect is known as a *moment*. The effect of a force depends on the distance from the fulcrum of the point at which the force acts. A force has a greater moment the further it is from the fulcrum.

The handlebars of a bicycle produce a turning effect about the steering column. The centre point, where the handlebars meet the column, is the fulcrum. The further apart the handlebar grips, the easier it is to turn the wheel and steer the bicycle. A see-saw is a lever system. The fulcrum is in the centre where the plank is supported. A bottle opener is a lever. The fulcrum of the system is the point at the end where the opener pivots and presses into the bottle top.

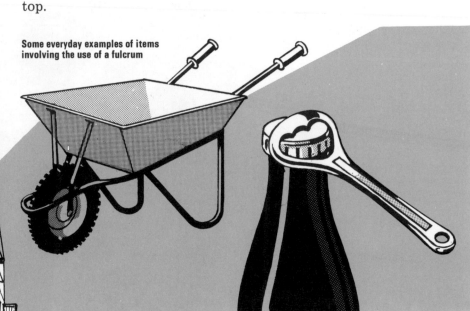

Some everyday examples of items involving the use of a fulcrum

What is equilibrium?

When two or more forces are acting against each other their combined effect may be to cancel each other out entirely. This means that the forces are in equilibrium.

On an old-fashioned set of kitchen scales, you put the food on one pan and the weights on the other. The two pans pivot about the fulcrum at the centre of the balance arm. To weigh the food, you add different weights until the scales balance; that is, the scales do not tip down to one side or the other. The forces acting on each side of the fulcrum are in equilibrium. Both forces have an equal turning effect about the pivot and cancel each other out. The value of one force is known; it is the total weight of the weights. The value of the other force is the same, so the weight of the food on the one side must be equal to that of the weights.

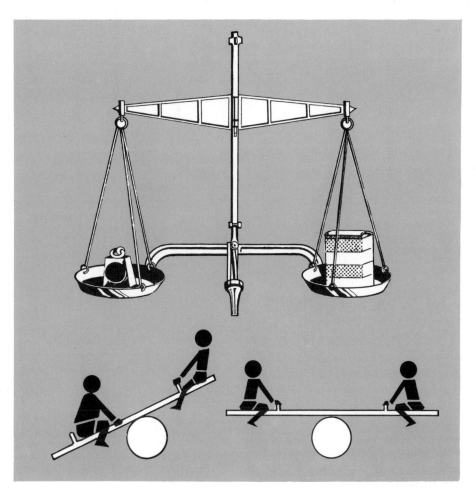

Why do we use levers?

A lever is one of the simplest types of machine. It provides men with a *mechanical advantage*. By applying a small force or effort to a lever, it can be used to overcome a larger force or load. This can be done because the turning effect of a force can be increased by applying it further away from the fulcrum, or pivot, of the system.

There are three different types or *classes*, of lever systems.

In the first-class lever system, such as a see-saw or a crow bar, the fulcrum is situated between the load and the effort. In a second class lever system such as a bottle opener, the load acts between the fulcrum and the effort. In a third class lever system, the effort acts between the load and the fulcrum.

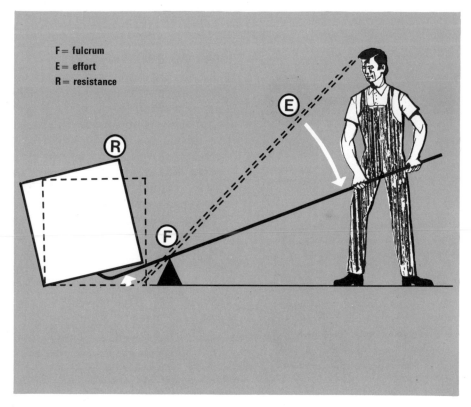

F = fulcrum
E = effort
R = resistance

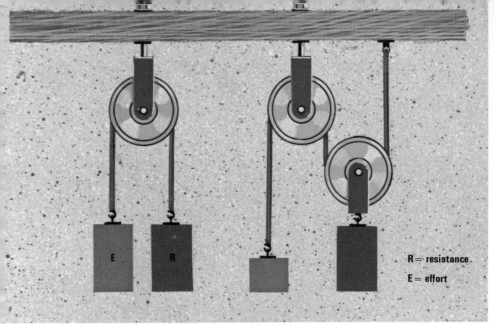

R = resistance
E = effort

Why do we use pulleys?

A pulley is another very simple machine, providing men with a mechanical advantage. By pulling down on the rope on one side of a pulley, a heavy weight can be lifted up the other side more easily than if it were being lifted straight up by hand. By using the pulley a man takes advantage of the downward pull of gravity on his body.

In a system of several pulleys, a large weight can be lifted by pulling on the rope with only a small force. But the weight will only rise a small distance compared with the distance the lifting force has to move in pulling the rope. The work done by the weight in moving up is equal to the work done by the lifting force in pulling out the rope.

In physics, the amount of work done by a force is equal to the size of the force multiplied by the distance it has moved. Pulley systems enable a small force to do enough work in moving a large distance, to move a larger force a smaller distance.

The efficiency of a machine is a measure of the amount of work put in compared to the amount of work got out. A machine is never quite one hundred percent efficient.

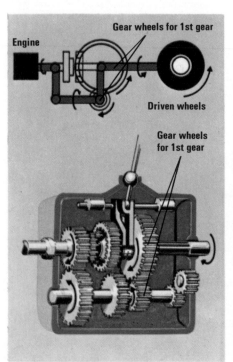

Engine

Gear wheels for 1st gear

Driven wheels

Gear wheels for 1st gear

How do gears work?

Gears are machines that can either convert a large force into a small one, or a small force into a large one.

If a force is applied to the teeth around the edge of the gear wheel, this force has a turning effect, or moment, about the centre of the gear wheel, where it rotates on a pin. The further the teeth are from the centre, the greater the effect of the force. Conversely, the gear wheel can be rotated at its centre by the axle, producing a force at the edge where the teeth strike anything.

By meshing the teeth of two gear wheels together, the force applied to one can be transferred to the other. If the teeth of the second wheel are further from its centre than those of the first wheel are from its centre, then the turning force on the second wheel will be greater than the first. If the second wheel is smaller, the effect of the force transmitted will be smaller.

Left: The top diagram shows the gear shafts of a car, while the lower one shows a gear box, with first gear engaged.

What is friction?

Friction is the force that acts between two moving surfaces that are touching each other. The force of friction tends to stop the movement.

How much friction there is between two surfaces depends on how rough they are; the rougher they are, the more friction there is. This can be reduced by *lubricating* the surfaces. Oil and grease are used as lubricants for metal surfaces such as those in motor car engines. The lubricant effectively fills in all the rough parts of the surface and provides a thin, smooth film for the other surface to slide over.

The amount of friction produced also depends on the force applied to the surfaces, either by the weight of the object if the gravity acts on it in a direction perpendicular to the surface, or by an external force.

Friction can stop movement, but it can also be useful in other ways. It enables surfaces to grip together. As a wheel rotates, it

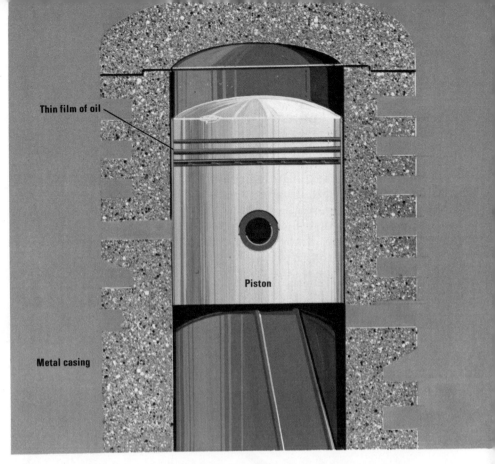

Thin film of oil

Piston

Metal casing

grips the ground at the bottom point where it touches, because of friction. If there is not enough friction, the wheel slips round and round. By placing a load on

wheels or rollers, an object that would have been difficult to slide because of too much friction, can be wheeled along because of just enough friction.

Why does hitting things make them hot?

Heat is a form of energy. It is not possible to create or destroy energy, it can only be changed from one form to another. The energy of movement, which is called kinetic energy, can be changed into heat.

The act of hitting an object, such as hammering a nail, involves using muscular energy to move the hammer. This energy is transferred suddenly to the nail at each blow. The energy given to the nail causes the molecules of iron to vibrate faster and the iron begins to heat up.

If you stop hitting the nail, the vibrations will gradually subside to their normal level.

Why do sliding things get hot?

When an object slides along a surface, it begins to get hot. This is caused by the friction between the object and the surface.

If you rub, or strike a match on a rough surface, it bursts into flames. This is because the head of the match has been dipped in a chemical substance that has a low *flash point*, that is, it catches alight, or *ignites* when it is heated up a little.

The heat is produced by the friction between the match and the rough surface.

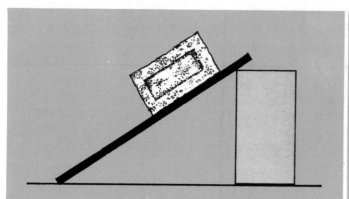

Why do rough things not slide easily?

The amount of friction between two surfaces depends on how rough they are. The rougher they are, the more friction there is. The amount of friction between two types of surface is known as the *coefficient* of friction.

Sometimes the friction may be so great that it overcomes the force moving the object. On icy railway lines, the ice sometimes makes the lines too smooth for an engine's wheels to get a grip. They just spin round uselessly. If gravel is thrown onto the line, this increases the friction between the wheels and the line. Conversely, if the wheels lock, they have to be dragged along the rail. If the friction is too great, the force pulling them may not be sufficient. So there must be some friction, but not too much.

What is viscosity?

The movement of a liquid is also slowed up as it moves across a surface, and flows through itself. This resistance to flow is called *viscosity*.

Fluids with high viscosity, such as syrup or heavy oil, flow more slowly than those with low viscosity, such as water.

The viscosity of a liquid can be lowered by warming it. This is easily seen when cooking oil is heated. It pours out thickly and forms a small, deep pool. As it warms up it spreads out thinly.

The viscosity of a gas increases when it is heated.

The different viscosities of liquids and gases make them useful as lubricants for various purposes.

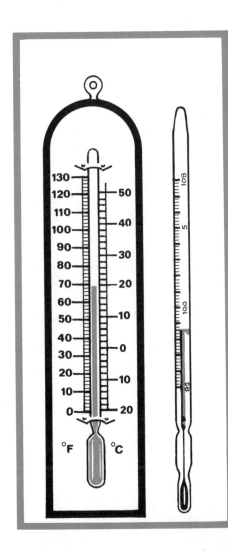

What is temperature?

The temperature of an object is a measure of its hotness. Heat is the energy possessed by an object due to the vibration of its molecules.

Temperature is measured by allowing the object to transfer some of its heat to a measuring instrument such as a thermometer. This instrument is *calibrated*, or previously marked, to indicate the change in it produced by a certain rise in temperature. In a thermometer this change is shown by a liquid that expands uniformly when it is heated, rising up a narrow tube marked with equal graduations.

A thermometer is marked off in divisions that indicate *degrees* of temperature. When the liquid rises up one division, the temperature has risen one degree.

There are several scales of temperature. On the Fahrenheit scale, the zero is equal to a temperature thirty two degrees below the freezing point of water (32°F). The boiling point of water is at 212°F. So there are 180 divisions, or degrees, between ice and steam. On the Centigrade or Celsius scale, the divisions, or degrees are larger. The freezing point of water indicates zero on the Celsius scale (0°C). The boiling point of water is 100°C. Another scale of temperature is the Kelvin scale. One Kelvin degree is equal to one Celsius degree, but the zeroes of the two scales are different. Zero on the Kelvin scale (0°K) is equal to —273·15°C. This is known as *absolute zero*.

The human body always maintains a steady temperature of 37°C (98·4°F) when it is healthy. We say that someone 'has a temperature' or is 'running a temperature' when their temperature rises a few degrees above this. They are probably seriously ill if it rises more than three degrees, or falls much below their normal temperature. Because the temperature of the human body is so critical, it is measured with a very delicate, accurate clinical thermometer, which can be read to show variations of a fraction of a degree.

Why do things feel cold?

When you touch something on a cold day that feels cold on your fingers, it is because it is at a lower temperature than your hand. It is conducting heat away from your hand quickly, because it is made of material that is a good conductor.

The two objects in contact, your hand and the cold object, are trying to reach a balanced state in which they are both at the same temperature.

On a warm day, the same object would feel warm, because good conductors heat up quickly. But something made of a different substance, that is a *bad* conductor, might still feel relatively cold on a warm day.

What is an insulator?

Wool, cork, polystyrene, fibreglass, plastic and rubber always feel quite warm, even in the coldest weather. Because of this, they are called good *insulators*.

Good insulators are bad conductors. They are very slow at conducting heat through them, passing the energy from molecule to molecule much less rapidly than a metal, for example.

This property is most useful for preventing heat from being lost too rapidly.

Water pipes, for example, are lagged with insulating material such as strips of felt or fibreglass, to prevent the water from freezing in winter.

Saucepan handles are made of insulating plastic material to prevent too much heat being conducted up from the pan and burning your hand.

What is a conductor?

On a warm day, if you touch a variety of objects, some of them will feel a lot warmer than others because they have absorbed more heat. The objects that heat up quickly, also cool down quickly. On a cold day they will feel colder than other objects.

Substances that respond quickly to heat are called good conductors. Most metals are good conductors, but glass, wood, cork, polystyrene and plastic are poor conductors.

The molecules in a substance are vibrating all the time. They vibrate faster when an object is warmed up. Some substances require less energy than others to make their molecules vibrate faster. These substances are good conductors.

Good conductors of heat are often good conductors of electricity too.

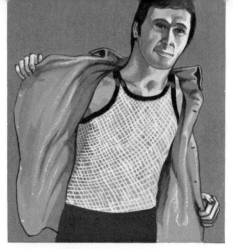

Why does a string vest keep you warm?

A string vest would certainly not keep you warm if you wore it by itself. You need to wear a shirt or sweater on top of it. The shirt traps a large amount of air next to your skin, in all the holes in the vest. Air is a good insulator. It does not conduct heat away from your body.

For the same reason, air does not allow heat to reach your body easily. So a string vest worn in hot weather will help to keep you cool.

Animals' fur and birds' feathers are both natural insulating 'clothing'. Air is trapped between the hairs of the fur or the layers of feathers. In cold weather, a bird fluffs out its feathers to trap a greater amount of air.

Why do gardeners use greenhouses?

To encourage young plants to grow quickly, they need warm, damp conditions. A greenhouse can provide this environment.

Greenhouses are made mostly of glass or transparent plastic to allow the maximum amount of sunlight to enter. It soon becomes very hot and humid inside because the heat of the Sun is trapped. The ventilation is controlled so that the moisture cannot evaporate away either, despite the heat.

Normally, hot air rises and in a house escapes out of windows, doors and chimneys. This is how heat travels by *convection*. But by keeping the door closed and only opening the windows when it gets too hot, the hot air is trapped.

The heat is not passed on to the air outside, because the glass or plastic sheets of which the walls are made, are bad conductors. So heat is not lost by *conduction*.

The only remaining way for the heat to travel is by *radiation*. The Sun's heat reaches the Earth in the form of *electromagnetic* waves which possess enormous amounts of energy. All objects *radiate* heat themselves, but they have absorbed some of the energy from the Sun's rays, to use it like fuel or food. The heat rays that plants send out have less energy than Sun rays. These heat rays do not have enough energy to pass through glass or plastic so heat is not lost by radiation.

How does double-glazing work?

Double-glazing prevents rooms with large windows from being too cold. It also helps to sound-proof a building.

Each window has two panes of glass sealed in a frame, so that air is trapped between them. Air is a bad conductor of heat, so whatever heat is conducted out of the room by the glass on the inside, is not easily transmitted to the outer pane. The air-filled space between the panes provides insulation, just as fibre-glass lagging does.

The air gap is also a poor transmitter of sound so that the double-glazing provides sound-proofing. Buildings on busy streets and near airports have double-glazing to keep out traffic noise. Recording studios have double-glazed windows so that a performance can be recorded without it being spoiled by outside noises.

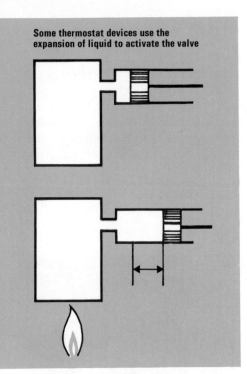

How does an oven thermostat work?

An oven thermostat is a mechanical device that is used on cooking stoves to keep the oven at a steady temperature for baking.

The thermostat contains a metal bar, which expands as the oven warms up. When the bar has expanded a certain amount, it switches the oven off by cutting off the fuel supply. In a gas oven it operates a valve that closes off the gas supply; in an electric oven the thermostat switches off the electric current. In oil-fired stoves, the oil supply is switched off and in solid fuel stoves, the thermostat reduces the draught by operating a switch that closes the dampers.

The thermostat can be set to any temperature by means of a regulo switch, which may have a temperature dial on it.

In some thermostats, the expanding metal bar is a bi-metallic strip. This is a strip made of two different types of metal, riveted together. The two metals have different rates of expansion. When the strip is heated up, it expands unevenly and begins to curve. This effect produces more mechanical movement than simply heating a small rod or bar, which only changes its length by a fraction.

Not only ovens require thermostats. Room thermostats can be fitted to regulate the central heating system. Industrial furnaces have their temperatures thermostatically controlled too.

How do dipping ducks keep moving?

Dipping ducks are old-fashioned toys that are a mystery, unless you know how they are made.

The duck is a dumbell-shaped bird, swinging on a pivot. You dip its beak in a glass of cold water and then allow it to swing freely.

It will swing backwards and forwards apparently endlessly, dipping its beak in the water from time to time.

The secret is the alcohol inside its body. The alcohol starts off as liquid in the lower, 'body' bulb. At room temperature, it gradually evaporates. It rises up the tube of the duck's neck and collects in the upper bulb, or head. The head gradually gets heavier with vapour, while the body gets lighter as the liquid evaporates. The duck swings further and further over on the pivot until its beak dips in the water. The beak is cooled immediately. The alcohol vapour in it condenses, and

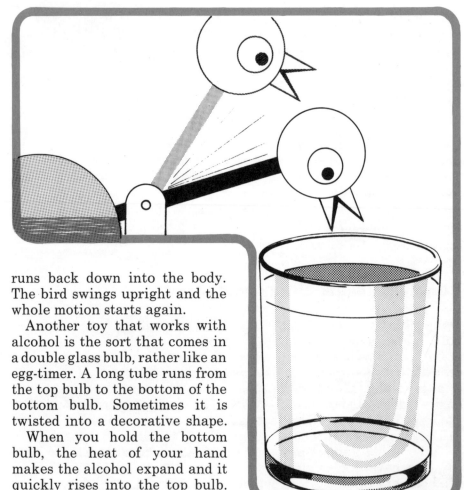

runs back down into the body. The bird swings upright and the whole motion starts again.

Another toy that works with alcohol is the sort that comes in a double glass bulb, rather like an egg-timer. A long tube runs from the top bulb to the bottom of the bottom bulb. Sometimes it is twisted into a decorative shape.

When you hold the bottom bulb, the heat of your hand makes the alcohol expand and it quickly rises into the top bulb. Let it cool, and it will run back.

How does a fridge work?

When a liquid evaporates and changes to a vapour, it uses up energy in the form of heat to make the change. It has to take the heat from its surroundings, so they grow cooler. This is how a refrigerator works.

The refrigerant, as it is usually called, is a liquid that can be changed to a gas, because it boils at a low temperature. Alternatively, it can be a gas that can easily be turned to a liquid, by putting it under pressure.

The usual substances used as refrigerants are ammonia or ethyl chloride.

A compressor puts the refrigerant under high pressure so that it becomes liquid because the molecules of gas are pressed together. This liquid circulates round the system and passes through a valve. On the other side of the valve, the pressure is lower. The liquid boils and turns back into a gas because its molecules are suddenly released from the pressure of the pump. It takes heat from its surroundings to do this and the refrigerator and its contents are cooled.

Food keeps better at low temperatures, because the bacteria which normally make it go bad, are unable to breed.

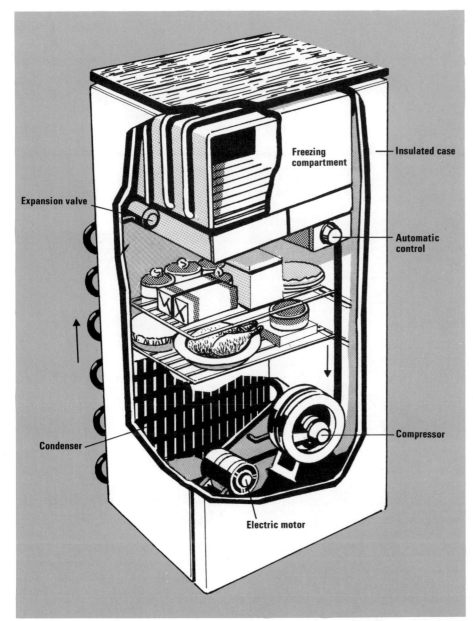

Expansion valve

Freezing compartment

Insulated case

Automatic control

Condenser

Compressor

Electric motor

Why do you blow on your hands to warm them, but on your soup to cool it?

When you blow on your hands on a cold day, your breath is warmer than your hands. Your cold skin absorbs heat from the hot air.

Steaming soup may be very nearly boiling, at a temperature near 100°C. Your breath is very much cooler than this. By blowing on the soup, you blow away the hot, steamy air above it, replacing it by cooler air from nearby. More heat escapes from the soup to warm up this air.

You can also alter the temperature of the air from your mouth. Breathe out with your mouth wide open. You can feel how warm the air is on your hand. Now whistle or blow with your lips almost closed. You can feel how much colder this air is.

It is the size of the hole that the air escapes from that affects the temperature. The smaller the hole, the more compressed is the escaping air. When a gas expands suddenly, it needs more energy. It takes it in in the form of heat, so its temperature, and that of its immediate surroundings, drops suddenly.

You will find this happening in several places: when you let go of a balloon and the air rushes out of the nozzle; when you open a compressed air line, used for inflating car tyres; when a train rushes out of a tunnel, and when steam escapes from a kettle.

How does a vacuum flask work?

A vacuum flask is a type of bottle in which liquids can be kept at a constant temperature. In a sealed vacuum flask, cold liquids stay cold and hot liquids stay hot.

The flask usually has an outer protective case, because the inner flask which holds the liquid is usually made of thin, delicate glass. This inner flask is also double-walled. The air is extracted from the space between the two thin walls to create a vacuum which is sealed off. No heat is conducted across a vacuum. Heat is thus prevented from escaping from the flask if the liquid is hot, or from entering the inner flask if the liquid is cold.

The glass walls are also silvered to reduce loss of heat by radiation. And because the walls are so thin, hardly any heat is lost by conduction.

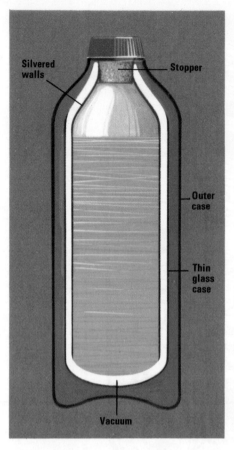

Why are teapots made shiny?

Natives of the temperate zones are not normally subjected to very much hot sunlight. The summers are short and the sun is not very hot. The people's skin is normally pale and white, but it can temporarily build up brown *pigment*. This is known as suntan. Excessive exposure to strong sun causes white skin to be sunburnt. This causes the top layer of skin to peel off in flakes, leaving fresh white skin underneath.

People of different races have different coloured skins, according to the climatic conditions in each race's natural environment. Natives from tropical climates have dark brown or black skins. Their skin contains a great deal of dark *pigment*. This protects their skin from harmful radiation in the strong sunshine.

Why do people in hot countries wear light coloured clothes?

In temperate climates such as that of Central Europe, people tend to wear light, bright, thin clothes in summer and darker, heavier, warmer clothes in winter. One of the reasons is probably that clothes get dirtier in the bad winter weather, and dark coloured cloth 'doesn't show the dirt'.

In hot climates, such as that of North Africa, the traditional costumes are long, white robes. The cloth is woven from light-coloured natural fibres. Coloured cloth is produced by dying the yarn, using natural dyes. The light coloured cloth is especially practical to wear because it is cooler to wear than a darker colour. For dark coloured surfaces not only radiate the most heat, but they also absorb heat more quickly than light coloured surfaces. The light cloth reflects back the rays of heat so that the wearer stays as cool as possible.

The clothes are usually loose fitting, to allow plenty of air to circulate round the body. This also helps the body to keep cool.

The houses in hot countries are often painted white too. If you walk up to a whitewashed wall in the sunshine, you can feel the heat being reflected off it, but inside it may remain quite cool.

Why does a fair person's skin go brown?

One of the ways in which a body cools down is by radiation. The heat is radiated from the body and warms the air around it.

The amount of heat a body radiates depends partly on its outer surface. Some types of surface radiate heat faster than others.

Rough dark surfaces radiate heat more quickly than smooth light coloured surfaces. This is why central heating radiators used to be painted black, although in modern homes the colour is now often chosen for its appearance.

Smooth, shiny surfaces radiate heat less quickly, which is why teapots are made with a polished metal surface, often of copper or silver. This helps the tea to stay hot.

Atoms move
above absolute zero

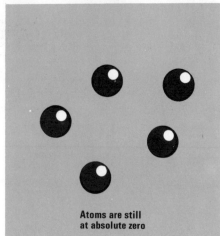

Atoms are still
at absolute zero

What is absolute zero?

The temperature of a body is always given in degrees.

The temperature scale used mainly in scientific work, is the Kelvin scale. One degree on the Kelvin scale is equal to one degree on the Celsius scale. But 0°C equals 273·15°K on the Kelvin scale. Zero on the Kelvin scale, 0°K, is equal to −273·15°C. This is known as absolute zero.

Different substances freeze, or become solid, at different temperatures. When a substance freezes, the molecules of which it is made up, vibrate at a much slower rate. The lower the temperature, the slower the vibrations. Eventually the molecules will stop vibrating altogether. This should take place when the temperature falls to 0°K, absolute zero. In practice this temperature has never been reached, although scientists have been able to drop the temperature of a substance to within a fraction of a degree above absolute zero.

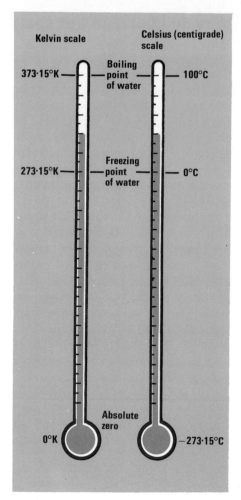

What is dry ice?

Dry ice is solid carbon dioxide. Carbon dioxide is normally found as a gas, in the atmosphere.

Dry ice is made by cooling and compressing carbon dioxide gas. This turns to a liquid. By blowing the liquid through a nozzle, its temperature drops even further, very quickly. This is because the pressure on it is lowered suddenly and rapidly as it sprays out of the nozzle into the atmosphere after being kept under pressure in the container. Some of the heat energy is converted into energy of movement as the expansion takes place. The drops of liquid carbon dioxide that spray out, solidify to form solid carbon dioxide 'snow'. The snow is packed together into blocks of dry ice.

Dry ice is much colder than ordinary water ice. It can be reduced to a temperature of −80°C. Because of its very low temperature, it will cause death if it is eaten, or if the snow is inhaled. It can 'burn' the skin if it is left in contact with it.

Dry ice is used as a refrigerant. It is especially useful for preserving food for transporting. Unlike ordinary ice, it does not melt and wet everything, it just evaporates away slowly. Nor does it contaminate the food, or goods. A van load of fish packed in dry ice will stay frozen for about five days. The containers are insulated to slow up the rate of evaporation. Dry ice is also used in medical research.

What is carbon monoxide?

Carbon monoxide is a poisonous gas. Its molecules are formed by the combination of one atom of carbon with one atom of oxygen. When the gas is burned, each molecule combines with another oxygen atom from the air, forming the common gas, carbon dioxide.

Carbon monoxide burns with a hot blue flame. It is one of the components of coal gas, which is used as domestic fuel in gas cookers and boilers, but in many places, a new type of gas is supplied that is not as poisonous.

The great danger of carbon monoxide is that it is colourless and has hardly any smell. A dangerous amount could leak out before being detected. Carbon monoxide poisoning causes unconsciousness and later, death, because the gas gets into the bloodstream. It combines with the haemoglobin in the red blood corpuscles, preventing them from carrying the life-giving oxygen to the brain.

Another dangerous source of carbon monoxide is in the exhaust fumes of motor engines. Carbon monoxide gas is also a serious hazard in coal mines, where its presence is continually monitored to prevent the risk of explosions.

What is carbon dioxide?

Whilst carbon monoxide is fatal to human life, carbon dioxide, with just one more atom of oxygen in each molecule, is vital to plants and animals.

Carbon dioxide is one of the gases found in the atmosphere. The gas we breathe out is carbon dioxide. Plants manufacture their food from carbon dioxide and water in the presence of sunlight. This process is called *photosynthesis*.

The element carbon is being continuously recycled through living organisms, back to the atmosphere, in the form of the carbon dioxide they give off. This is called the *carbon cycle*.

Carbon dioxide will not burn, and it is heavier than air, so it is used in fire extinguishers.

Above: At night, plants lined up in a greenhouse give off carbon dioxide. This is to make room for the oxygen that they absorb. During the day, this process is reversed.

Where does nitrogen come from?

Nitrogen occurs as a gas in the atmosphere, of which it makes up the major part. Air contains about 78 percent nitrogen. It is a fairly inactive gas, but the element nitrogen is essential to living organisms. Plants obtain nitrogen in the form of inorganic nitrogen compounds. These are drawn out of the soil by their roots. The plants convert these compounds into proteins, in which form animals can absorb them.

Both plants and animals return the nitrogen they absorb, to the soil, in the form of waste matter, decaying plants and the bodies of dead animals. Bacteria convert the nitrogen compounds these contain, back into a form in which plants can absorb them again.

Bacteria cause nitrogen to be returned to the atmosphere. The action of lightning also causes a transfer of nitrogen from the atmosphere to the earth.

This continuous cyclic movement of nitrogen from one form to another is known as the nitrogen cycle.

Nitrogen occurs naturally as the compound *Chile saltpetre*.

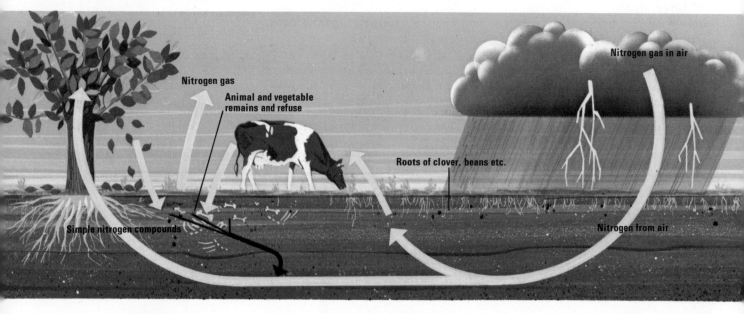

Nitrogen gas in air

Nitrogen gas

Animal and vegetable remains and refuse

Roots of clover, beans etc.

Simple nitrogen compounds

Nitrogen from air

What are the 'bends'?

The 'bends' are caused by bubbles of nitrogen forming in a person's bloodstream and body tissue. This is a dangerous condition which can be fatal.

The bubbles of nitrogen form when the air pressure surrounding a person's body is suddenly lowered. This can happen when a diver rises quickly to the surface after being subjected to high pressures underwater. It is avoided by making the journey to the surface in several stages, allowing the body time to adjust to the rising pressure. The diver must pause for several minutes at regular intervals, or use an air-lock in which the pressure can be altered by means of a pump. Pilots can also get an attack of the 'bends' if they ascend to high altitudes too quickly, without protection against the lower pressure.

The bends are cured by immediately placing the person in a pressure chamber, raising it to the pressure he had got used to, and then lowering the pressure to normal, gradually. The risk of the bends is reduced by using breathing apparatus that supplies pure oxygen, immediately prior to, and during an ascent. This removes a large amount of nitrogen from the body and reduces the danger of bubbles forming.

What is air?

Air is the name given to the collection of gases that make up our atmosphere. Air is composed mainly of the gas nitrogen (78%). The second most plentiful gas is oxygen (21%), the gas that we breathe in. All the other gases together amount to only one percent. These include carbon dioxide (the gas we breathe out).

Air is essential to life. Plants manufacture their food from carbon dioxide. Animals need a supply of oxygen for their brains to function.

Air is also essential to combustion and burning. A flame needs oxygen to keep it alight.

The composition of air varies from place to place, and the air in our atmosphere is constantly moving. The movement of air currents or winds gives us our changing weather. At high altitudes the air is 'thinner' or less dense. It does not contain enough oxygen for men to breathe, so high altitude mountaineers and pilots use special breathing apparatus.

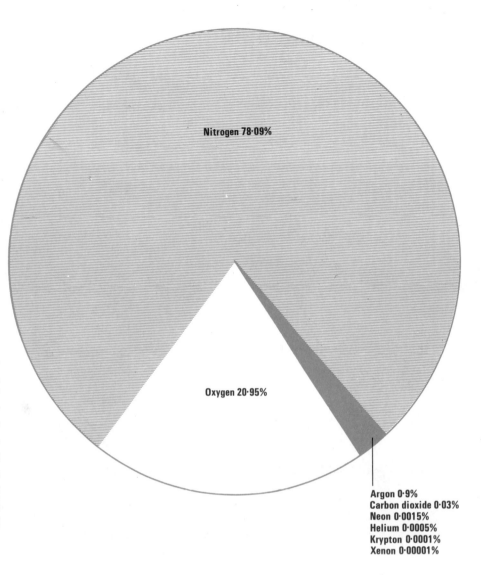

Nitrogen 78·09%

Oxygen 20·95%

Argon 0·9%
Carbon dioxide 0·03%
Neon 0·0015%
Helium 0·0005%
Krypton 0·0001%
Xenon 0·00001%

What is lighter than air?

Both hydrogen and helium are lighter than air. If a balloon is inflated with either of these gases, and released, it will float up into the atmosphere, because it is 'lighter than air'. Some of the airships that were used for air transport at the beginning of this century, were filled with hydrogen. Because hydrogen is highly inflammable, the slightly heavier gas, helium is now used instead.

Aircraft used to be called 'lighter-than-air-machines'. However, aircraft do not rise into the air because they are light, but because of the way the air flows over their wings, producing a lifting force.

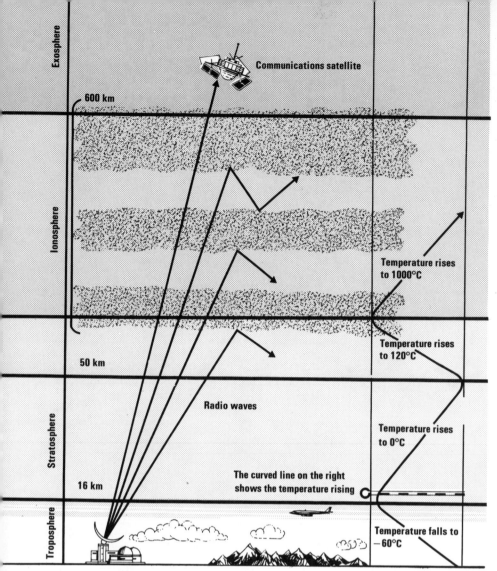

Communications satellite

600 km

Exosphere

Ionosphere

Temperature rises to 1000°C

50 km

Temperature rises to 120°C

Radio waves

Stratosphere

Temperature rises to 0°C

16 km

The curved line on the right shows the temperature rising

Troposphere

Temperature falls to −60°C

What is the atmosphere?

The atmosphere is the envelope of air that surrounds the Earth. Apart from the mixture of gases that make up air, the atmosphere also contains water vapour, some hydrocarbons, hydrogen peroxide, compounds of sulphur and dust particles, all in relatively small amounts.

There are four distinct layers in the atmosphere. Next to the Earth's surface, and stretching up to a height of about sixteen kilometres is the troposphere. The temperature in the troposphere generally falls the higher you go. Above this is the stratosphere, rising to a height of about fifty kilometres. Here the temperature rises again. Above the stratosphere is the deepest layer, the ionosphere, rising to a height of 600 kilometres. The temperature falls and rises again, sharply to over 1000°C. In the ionosphere are bands of particles that reflect radio waves back to Earth.

Beyond the ionosphere is the exosphere. This merges into outer space.

What is pollution?

One of the most serious problems in the modern world is pollution. Man's way of life, his agriculture and his industry are spoiling this planet.

Most of our activities involve waste products and these are scattered over the land. They are polluting, or spoiling, the soil, water and air. As the population in an area increases, the problem becomes more and more serious.

By overworking the land, all the goodness is removed from the soil. In some areas the soil has changed its texture so that it is now blown away as dust. Pesticides, fungicides and chemical waste poison plant life; animals are poisoned too, or starve to death. The effluent, or waste from factories, makes river water unfit to drink. Oil slicks pollute the sea and smother the beaches. Millions of motor cars and furnaces are filling the atmosphere with poisonous fumes and dust.

Methods of reducing pollution are being used in many places. Scientific methods are applied to farming. Waste, instead of being thrown away, is being recycled. Effluent is purified before being released into the water. Smokeless fuels and filters reduce atmospheric pollution.

What is a vacuum?

A vacuum is a space which does not contain any molecules or atoms. It is impossible to obtain a perfect vacuum, but a very high vacuum can be obtained with a special machine.

The atmospheric pressure in a vacuum is very, very minute. Natural forces all work towards preventing a vacuum from forming, by filling up the space with matter. Air flows, or is sucked into a vacuum when the vacuum seal is released, until finally the air pressure is the same throughout the system.

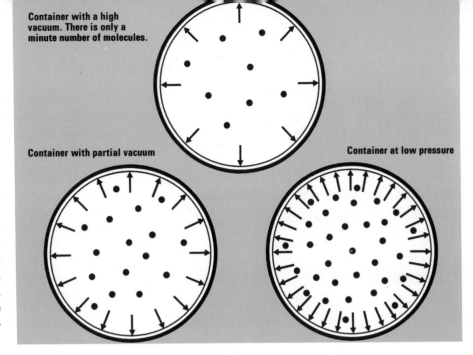

Container with a high vacuum. There is only a minute number of molecules.

Container with partial vacuum

Container at low pressure

What is a vacuum cleaner?

A vacuum cleaner is a domestic electrical appliance used to pick up small pieces of dirt and dust. It contains a powerful electric fan that sucks air into the machine quickly, blowing it through a filter and out in another direction. The sudden removal of the air at the front of the machine tends to create a vacuum. However, nature prevents this by quickly filling the space inside the machine with air from the immediate surroundings.

The suction force is so great, that small particles of dust and dirt are drawn in with the air and are collected inside the cleaner. This makes the work of extracting grit and dust from between the fibres of a carpet much easier than brushing or sweeping it up.

What is a vacuum seal?

Many of the goods we buy today are vacuum sealed. This is especially true of food packets, for the food must be kept fresh. It also applies to products that must be kept dry and to sterilize hospital equipment, too.

A vacuum seal closes the object in a partial vacuum. A small amount of air is drawn out before the container is closed. This means that the pressure on the outside of the container is greater than the pressure on the inside. The greater pressure keeps the lid or sealed edges pressed down tightly.

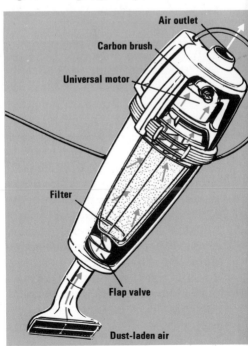

Air outlet

Carbon brush

Universal motor

Filter

Flap valve

Dust-laden air

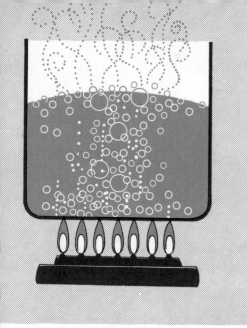

Why does boiling water bubble?

If you watch a pan of water very closely as it comes to the boil, you can see the bubbles forming. They begin as tiny specks, sparkling on the bottom of the pan, slowly growing into dome-shaped bubbles. These rise from the bottom, turning into sphere-shaped bubbles, rising quickly to the surface in a constant stream. As the bubbles rise they grow larger and larger, until they reach the surface, where they burst.

These are bubbles of air that were trapped in the water and compressed until they were too small to see. As the water is heated, the air in it expands more quickly than the liquid. Because the bubbles of air are less dense than the liquid, they rise, driven upwards by convection currents in the liquid.

As they rise to the surface, the pressure of water on the bubbles decreases and they grow larger. The bubbling becomes more intense as the water nears boiling point.

Why does it seem warmer at the sea by night than in the daytime?

A cool wind usually blows in off the sea, even on a hot, sunny day. This is the sea breeze. It is caused by *convection currents*. These are currents of hot air circulating in the atmosphere.

On the evening of the same day, after the Sun has set, it may seem surprisingly warm by the sea's edge. The sea breeze has dropped and in fact has been replaced by a breeze off the land. The convection currents are now circulating in the opposite way.

This change is caused by the different rates at which the land and the water heat up and cool down. The Sun heats land up more quickly than water, because rock and earth are better conductors of heat than water. For the same reason, the land loses its heat more quickly, after sunset.

So for most of the day, the water is cooler than the land, and the air above the sea is warmed only a little by the water. The air above the land is warmed more than the air above the sea. The hot air rises, setting up convection currents, and a current of cool air flows in from the sea to replace the rising warm air. This is the sea breeze.

At night the land cools down more quickly than the sea. So the air above the sea is warmed more than that above the land. The air above the sea rises higher, so air flows in off the land to replace it. This is the land breeze. The direction of the convection currents has been reversed.

At some stage in the morning, just after sunrise, and in the evening around sunset, the temperatures of the land and the sea are roughly equal. The air temperature is also about the same above both, so there is no flow of cool air from one place to another. The breeze ceases, the ripples on the sea die away and there is the typical calm of a fine evening or morning. Smoke drifts straight upwards and flags hang limp.

Below: The diagram on the left shows the direction of a sea breeze, and on the right is a land breeze.

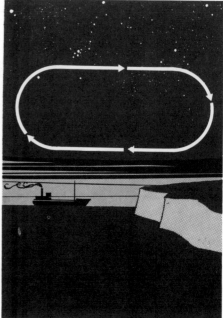

Why does hot air rise?

When a mass of air, or any gas is heated it expands, if it is not in an enclosed space. The molecules vibrate more energetically and move further apart, so there is less matter in a given volume than there is in a colder mass of gas. The hot gas is less dense than the colder gas, so it begins to rise. In fact it is the colder, more dense gas, which sinks, or is drawn in from around the sides.

A continuous upward flow of hot air is set up, called a *convection current*.

Convection currents play an important part in our weather. Convection currents keep the air in a room circulating. You can sometimes see the 'heat waves' dancing over the hot plate of a stove, or even on the road surface on a very hot day.

What causes draughts?

However hot the fire you are sitting by, you nearly always feel a draught. Normally you feel it around your feet, or down your neck.

The draught at your feet is cold air being drawn in under the door, or through gaps in the floorboards, if there are any.

The draught down your neck is probably cold air coming in from around the window.

The draughts are caused by the *convection currents* that the fire sets up. It heats the air in front of it. This rises, mainly up the chimney, and cold air is drawn in from outside the room to replace it.

To keep the air in a room fresh and well ventilated, it is important to have a top window open for the warmer, stale air to escape from. A lower window should also be open for cool fresh air to be drawn in.

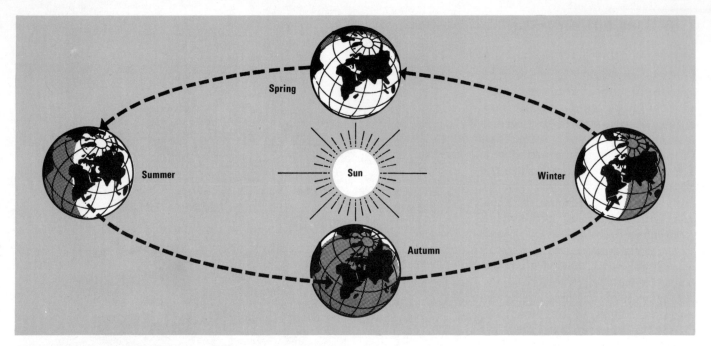

Why do we have seasons?

The Earth spins round on its axis, completing one revolution a day. At the same time, it is travelling round the Sun, taking one year to make a complete revolution. The Earth's axis is tilted at an angle to its orbit. This means that at some positions in its orbit each part of the Earth's surface spends more time facing the Sun than it does when the Earth is in another part of its orbit. This produces the effect known as the seasons.

It is the summer season, or solstice, in the part of the Earth that is facing the Sun for the longest time each day, and has the shortest night. That part then moves into the autumn season, or equinox, as the days get shorter and nights grow longer. Winter is the season when the days are shortest and the nights are longest.

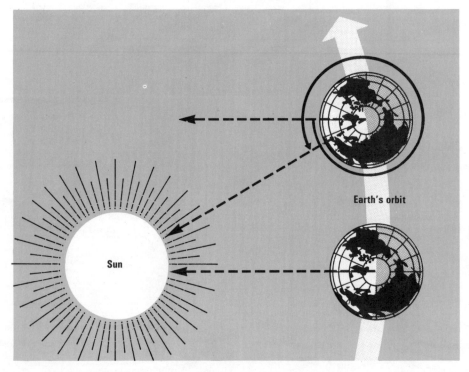

Why do we have leap year?

An ordinary year is 365 days long. This is the number of whole days that it takes for the Earth to complete an orbit around the Sun. But in fact it takes just a little longer than that by a quarter of a day. It would be impractical to have a year of $365\frac{1}{4}$ days, so we have an extra day every fourth year, which is known as leap year. The extra day is added onto the shortest month, February, giving us 29 February.

If no adjustment were made, our calendar would not keep in time with the seasons. Midsummer in the northern hemisphere would eventually fall in December.

How is a pendulum used to tell the time?

The regular behaviour of a simple pendulum provides man with a means of measuring the passage of time. For however heavy the weight, and whether the swings are very tiny or quite wide, it always takes the same length of time to complete one swing.

To change the period, or time taken for a swing you must change the length of the string or wire. The shorter the string, the shorter the time of swing.

By linking this perfectly regular movement of a pendulum through a gear mechanism, the hands of a clock are moved round the dial at a regular pace.

It is said that the famous Italian scientist, Galileo Galilei, noticed that a pendulum behaves in this fashion, when he was watching a lamp swinging from the roof of the cathedral.

Same time of swing

Faster

Slower

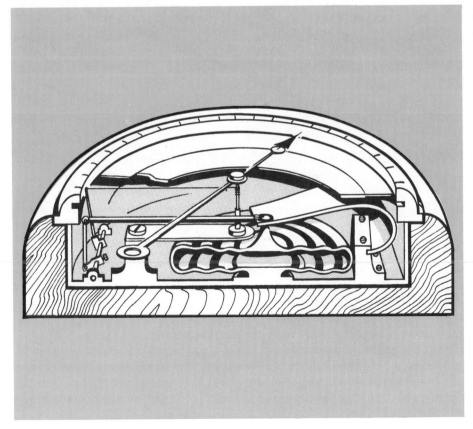

How does a barometer forecast the weather?

A barometer is an instrument that measures the pressure of the gases in the atmosphere.

When the atmospheric pressure is steady, the weather is usually settled and fine. When the atmospheric pressure rises, it heralds hot, dry weather. When the pressure falls, there is likely to be wet, cold weather. The lower the pressure, the less water vapour the air is able to hold. The surplus falls as rain.

A barometer indicates what the atmospheric pressure is at any moment in time. By watching the changes, the type of weather approaching an area can be predicted.

Left: Most modern barometers are made of a hermetically sealed box, which has no air inside.

Where does light come from?

The particles that make up all atoms are continually moving, colliding and exchanging energy. Some of this energy is sent out, or emitted from the atom in the form of electromagnetic radiation. Our eyes are sensitive to a certain form of this radiation, which we call light.

Light comes to the Earth from the Sun and, in much more minute quantities, from the stars. Moonlight is sunlight that has been reflected to Earth from the surface of the Moon.

Natural sources of light on Earth are from fire, lightning, and from *phosphorescent* substances.

There are many methods of producing artificial light. In olden times they burned oil and wax candles; then gas lighting was invented.

Now we have all sorts of different kinds of electric lighting and gas-discharge lamps.

What is light?

Light always travels in straight lines. As a result, it causes sharp shadows to be formed where the edge of an object cuts off the light suddenly.

Light is a type of electromagnetic radiation, and this is a form of energy, radiated from atoms, that travels in waves. These waves can be of different *frequencies*. The frequency is the rate at which the pulses of energy are vibrating. At the same time, the radiation can be of different wavelengths. The length of a wave is the distance between the topmost two wavecrests.

The faster the vibrations, the higher the frequency and the shorter the wavelength.

Visible light is electromagnetic radiation within a particular range of frequencies and the corresponding wavelengths. The whole range of frequencies of the electromagnetic radiation is called the electromagnetic spectrum. The part of the range to which our eyes are sensitive is called the visible spectrum.

We see a bright, white mixture of all radiation at all frequencies within the visible spectrum, and call it light.

All electromagnetic waves travel through empty space at a speed of almost three hundred million metres per second. This is known as the speed of light. On Earth, light travels through all sorts of different substances which slows it down. The change in the speed at which it travels causes a beam of light to change direction. This is known as refraction.

Substances that allow light to pass through them easily are called *transparent*. Those that do not let light through at all are called *opaque*.

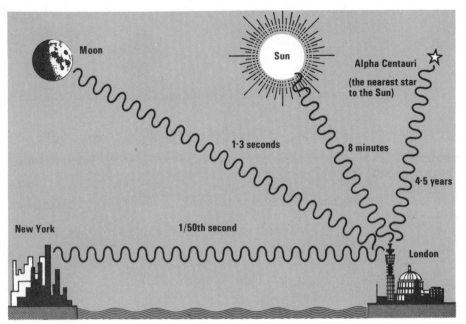

Left: The speed of light.

Labels in image: Moon, Sun, Alpha Centauri (the nearest star to the Sun), 1·3 seconds, 8 minutes, 4·5 years, New York, 1/50th second, London

What is a light year?

The stars are so far away that it is not practical to measure their distance in terrestrial units of length. Instead they are measured in the astronomical unit of light years. A light year is the distance travelled by light in one year.

Light travels through space at a speed of three hundred thousand kilometres per second (300,000 km/sec). There are over three million seconds in a year. So a light year is over nine million, million kilometres.

Can we travel as fast as light?

Experiments have shown that if an object could be made to travel as fast as light, our normal time process would be slowed down. On Earth we find this almost impossible to imagine and although it sounds like 'science fiction', it is, in fact, true!

The mass of an object moving very fast changes as it nears the speed of light, and the rate at which time passes also changes. A man who was travelling inside a space-craft would be quite unaware of these changes around him; but to someone on Earth, the astronaut's watch would appear to be running slower than normal and he would not be ageing so quickly.

Once a space-craft reaches the speed of light, time would literally stand still. If an astronaut on such a flight left the Earth as a middle-aged man, leaving his young son behind, when he returned many years later, he would not be much older himself but his young son would already be an old, old man.

Left: Light travels in waves that can be of different frequencies. If we could see these waves, they might look like the waves in a rope.

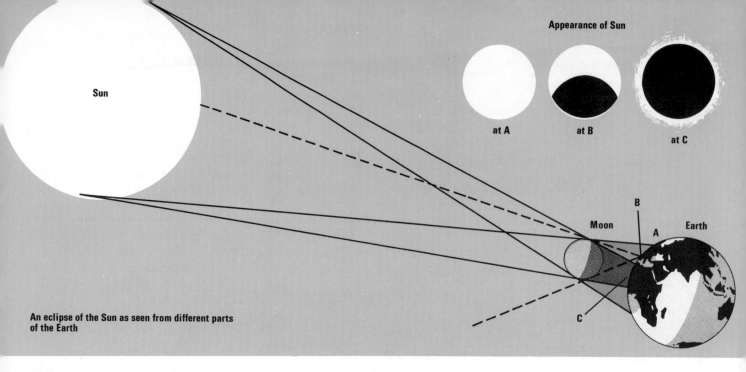

Sun

Appearance of Sun

at A

at B

at C

B

Moon

A

Earth

C

An eclipse of the Sun as seen from different parts of the Earth

What is starlight?

Scientists believe that starlight is like the light from our Sun, which is also a star. But the other stars appear as no more than tiny pin-pricks because they are an enormous distance away from the Earth.

They are so far away that the light reaching us now from a close star group, the Andromeda Nebula, must have left those stars two million years ago.

The theory of how the light is produced is that a violent reaction is taking place within each star. Hydrogen, which is the lightest element, is converted to helium, which is the next lightest element. This involves the release of vast amounts of radiant energy that travels out in every direction. The radiation travels at the speed of light, and our eyes are sensitive to part of it; that is, those parts that have wavelengths that lie within the visible spectrum.

The stars only appear to shine in the sky at night, because during the day, the Sun is so bright that we cannot detect the much fainter starlight.

The so-called morning and evening stars are in fact planets, which are much closer to the Earth than any of the stars, as they are part of the solar system.

The stars seem to twinkle because of the moving layers of particles in the atmosphere. These break up and scatter the radiation from the stars, making them appear to vary in brightness.

The same thing happens to sunlight on a larger scale, when you travel quickly past a line of trees. You see only the interrupted rays of sunlight, and so the sunlight appears to twinkle.

The stars will go on shining for millions of years, but eventually they will probably run out of 'fuel' and burn out. But by the time we stop receiving the light from them, they will have been dead for a few million years already.

74

What causes an eclipse?

An eclipse is caused when the orbit of the Moon round the Earth brings it between the Sun and the Earth. When this happens it blocks out all or part of the Sun's light, so that it disappears from view. If the Moon blocks out the whole of the Sun it is called a total eclipse; if it only blocks out a part, it is called a partial eclipse.

Early man did not understand how eclipses were caused nor could he tell when they were going to happen as we can today. Usually he worshipped the Sun, and when the Sun disappeared he thought something evil was eating it away. Sometimes a religious ceremony would take place to drive away the evil. Of course, this always seemed successful, as the Moon moved across the Sun, which then could be seen shining again.

There are also eclipses of the Moon. The light we see from the Moon is light from the Sun reflected off the Moon's surface. An eclipse of the Moon happens when the Earth itself comes between the Sun and the Moon. The Earth therefore cuts off the light before it reaches the Moon.

Below: A total eclipse of the Sun. The Sun's surface is completely blotted out, but the corona can still be seen, extending far out beyond the Sun's surface. The corona is the layer of extremely hot gas.

Why should you always wear dark glasses to watch an eclipse?

The inside of the eyeball is covered with a layer known as the retina. This is covered in millions of tiny, light-sensitive cells called rods and cones. The retina is very sensitive and can be damaged if it is exposed to too much high-energy radiation. This can result in temporary, or even permanent, blindness.

Normally, you cannot look at the bright Sun for more than a moment, because it hurts your eyes. Involuntarily, you feel yourself 'screwing up' your eyes into narrow slits, to let in as little light as possible. This is one of the natural protective mechanisms that nature has given you to protect your eyes.

The power radiation from the Sun can damage the eyes. Fortunately, the atmosphere filters out a great deal of the most harmful radiation, but some still gets through and so the eyes have to be shielded from it.

During an eclipse, the Moon passes across the face of the Sun,

Corona

Chromosphere

blocking out much of the light. This is not a very frequent occurrence and attracts people's curiosity. It is quite easy to look up at the darkened Sun, but it is extremely dangerous. Although there is not as much light, there is still more than enough of the invisible high-energy radiation to damage the eyes. Therefore, eclipses should be studied with great care, using good eye protection such as polaroid glasses. It used to be common to watch them through a piece of smoked glass that had been blackened with candle soot, but this is not

sufficient.

Strong sunlight can be dangerously powerful when reflected, too. Reflections off water and snow especially, can cause damage. Snow-blindness is very painful. It is also very deceptive because you do not know it has happened until about twelve hours after the exposure has occurred. The vision first becomes misty and may then be lost entirely. At the same time there is an agonizing sensation of extreme irritation in the eyes. The person has to be kept quiet until normal vision returns.

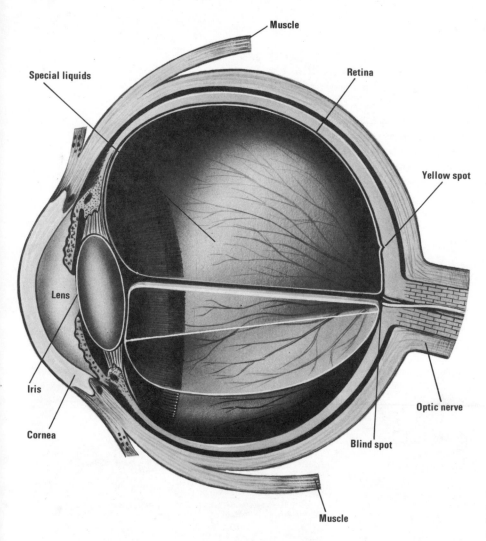

Muscle

Special liquids

Retina

Yellow spot

Lens

Iris

Cornea

Optic nerve

Blind spot

Muscle

How do we see things?

Each of your eyes is shaped like a ball. At the front of the eye is a transparent outer layer called the cornea. The coloured part is called the iris; this is the part you are talking about when you say a person has blue, brown, green or hazel eyes. In the middle of the iris is a hole called the pupil. This appears black but it is really this which lets in the light so that you can see.

The iris acts as a screen over the lens. When there is plenty of light, for example on a sunny day, the iris closes up because you do not need all the light which is around to see by. When it is darker the iris gets much smaller so that more light is let into the eye and you can see better.

The light coming into your eye contains an image. When it has

Below: The boy in the picture is looking at the flowers through one eye only, so that he sees them in two dimensions. Try this yourself, and then notice the difference when you use both eyes.

How do we see things in three dimensions?

We see things in three dimensions because we have two eyes. Each eye sees a slightly different view of an object so that we see not just the front of an object, but slightly down each side. This gives us a rounded view of things and makes them appear solid.

A photograph looks flat because it is only two-dimensional. If we had only one eye, like the camera has only one lens, we would only see in two dimensions. Look down the length of a matchbox held about 50 centimetres from your eyes; if you close one eye you can see the end and one side but with both eyes open you can see both sides.

You can prove that each of your eyes sees things from a different viewpoint. Close one eye and hold a finger up in line with a thin object, such as a ruler some distance away. Close that eye and open the other one still holding the finger in the same position. You will find the ruler is no longer in line with your finger.

The fact that we see in three dimensions makes it easy, too, for us to judge the relative distance of objects. If you hold your hands apart with one finger from each pointing towards the other, it is perfectly easy to touch the two fingers together in front of you with both eyes open, but quite difficult with one eye open.

entered your eye, the light passes through a lens which focuses the image onto the retina. The retina is the wall on the inside of the eye.

The lens has muscles around it. These automatically change the shape of the lens so that the image on the retina is in focus. If you look at a close object and then look away to a distant view, the view will seem blurred for a moment. This is the time it takes for the lens in your eye to change its shape and focus the image onto the retina properly.

The cells of the retina convert the light into electrical messages which are carried to the brain by the optic nerve. The images focused on the retina are upside-down, but the brain automatically turns the image the right way up in our minds.

Why do different animals have their eyes positioned in different parts of their heads?

Because of the different way in which they live, animals need to use their eyes for different purposes. As evolution has progressed, the eyes of each type of animal have gradually come to be in the part of the head where they are most useful.

If an animal's eyes are set straight in the front of it's face, this enables it to focus clearly on one spot and to judge distance accurately. This is very useful to animals that live by hunting, such as cats, foxes and owls.

Animals such as the rabbit, which is hunted by other animals but eats vegetation, do not need to see so clearly in front. It is more important that they can see over a wide area. A rabbit's eyes are set back, to the sides of its head, near the top, so that it can quickly look to the sides, behind and above it.

Frogs and hippopotamuses have eyes set high up near the tops of the head so that they can see above the water when they are partly submerged.

In the picture above, three animals can be seen with eyes in totally different positions.

How does a telescope work?

The human eye cannot see distant objects clearly. The telescope is an instrument used by sailors, marksmen, astronomers and many others, to view distant objects in detail.

There are two main types of telescope, the *refractor* and the *reflector*.

In the refractor, the light from a distant object is refracted by the glass in the objective lens. This brings it to a focus at the focal point of a second lens or eyepiece, through which the image is viewed.

One of the earliest refracting telescopes was devized by Galileo, but the poor quality of the lenses at that time did not make the image very sharp.

The reflecting telescope produces a better image. It uses a curved mirror to produce the image which is reflected from a second mirror and viewed through an eyepiece lens. Sir Isaac Newton invented the Newtonian reflecting telescope.

Above right: The boy in this picture is using a refracting telescope.

Centre: A refracting telescope, showing the objective lens and the eyepiece.

Right: The principle of both the Galilean telescope (*above*) and Kepler's astronomical telescope (*below*). In Galileo's telescope a concave lens is used, so that the image seen is the right way up. Kepler's on the other hand, uses a convex eyepiece, producing an upside down image.

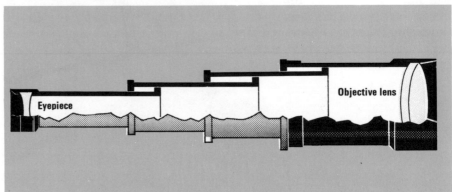

Eyepiece

Objective lens

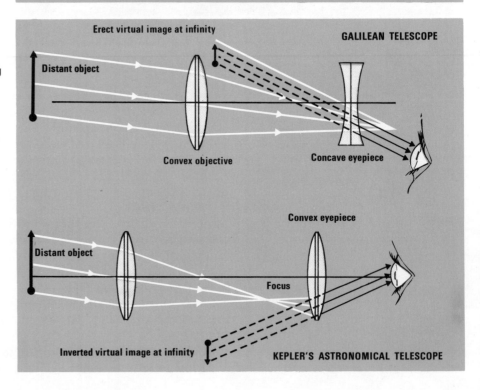

Erect virtual image at infinity

GALILEAN TELESCOPE

Distant object

Convex objective

Concave eyepiece

Convex eyepiece

Distant object

Focus

Inverted virtual image at infinity

KEPLER'S ASTRONOMICAL TELESCOPE

How do spectacles help people to see?

Some people cannot focus objects that are close to them. We say they are long-sighted.

Others can only see objects clearly if they are very close indeed. We say they are short-sighted, or *myopic*.

These defects of vision may happen because the lenses of the eyes cannot change shape sufficiently to focus the rays on the retina. This is the light-sensitive surface on the inside of the eyeball. The muscles may be too weak or the eyeball may be misshapen.

For short-sighted people, the image is normally brought to a focus at a point before it reaches the retina. This can be corrected by wearing spectacles with con-

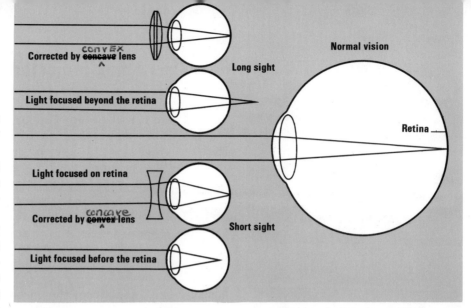

cave diverging lenses. These bend the rays outwards, so that the object appears to be nearer, where the short-sighted eye is able to focus as it would naturally.

For people with long sight, the point at which the lens would bring light rays from an object

into focus, would be behind the eyeball if that were possible. By wearing spectacles with convex, converging lenses, this distance is reduced so that they are focused on the retina. The long-sighted person is then able to see objects at all distances quite clearly.

How does a microscope magnify?

A simple microscope has only a single lens system which will magnify objects that can already be seen with the naked eye.

Compound microscopes have two sets of lenses, the objective and the eyepiece, fixed at opposite ends of a tube. The tube is raised or lowered, above the object on the microscope slide, bringing the highly magnified image into focus. The objective, at the lower end of the tube, magnifies the image first and the eyepiece magnifies this to give an even larger image. Eyepieces and objectives of different magnifications can be used.

Below: The human eye (A) can separate dots 0·25 mm. apart. The light microscope (B) can separate dots 0·25 microns apart and the electron microscope (C) can separate dots less than 5 Angstrom units apart. (A micron is 0·001 mm. and an Angstrom unit is 0·001 microns.)

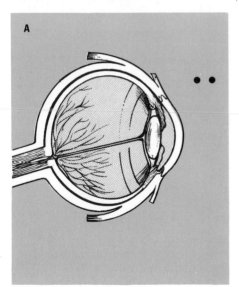

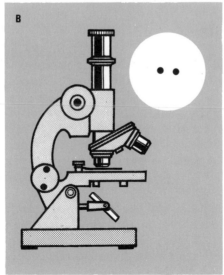

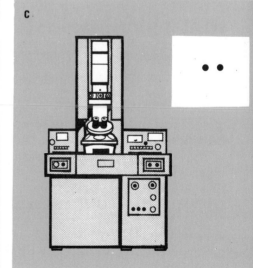

How does a cine-projector work?

A cine-projector contains a lamp which shines through a lens. The strip of film runs between the lamp and the lens which magnifies and focuses the tiny image on the film. This is projected onto a screen, so that the viewers see a clear picture.

A cinefilm is made up of a series of small pictures. When the camera is used to take a picture of something moving, such as a horse, it does not film the horse continuously, but takes a lot of separate pictures in quick succession. Most modern cameras take eighteen pictures per second.

The film is run through the projector at exactly the same speed as it ran through the camera. One might expect the pictures to be jerky as the film moves from one shot to the next. This does not happen because the image from the screen stays on the *retina* at the back of the watching person's eye, until the next picture is seen. The human eye cannot see separate images if they are presented less than about one twelfth of a second apart. Some very old films look too fast and jerky if they are shown with a modern projector.

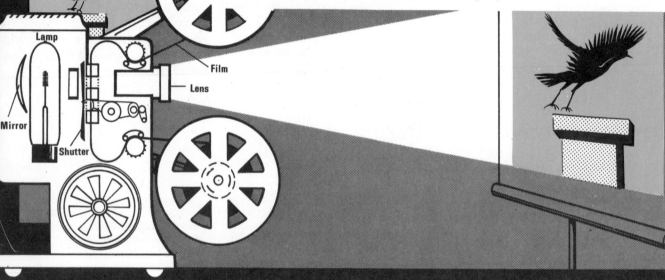

What is a stroboscopic picture?

The eye takes a fraction of a second to see an object and register it in the brain. If the object moves very fast, such as a dancer spinning round, it looks like a blurr.

If a fast flashing light is shone on the subject, for a brief fraction of a second, it is seen in one position for that moment of time. At the next flash, the subject will already have reached another position.

The kind of light used for this is called a stroboscope. Moving objects lit by one of them jump, apparently jerkily, from one position to another.

If the object is moving round and round, and the flashes are timed, or *synchronized*, to coincide with each revolution, the object will appear to stand still. If the flashes are a fraction faster than the rate of revolution, it will appear to spin backwards, because the object has not quite moved round to the start by the next flash.

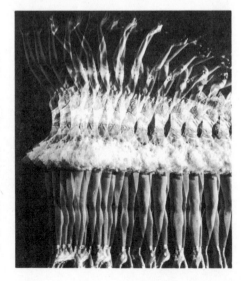

Why do we see spots before the eyes?

'Spots before the eyes' are what is known as an *after image*. They happen after you have been looking at a pattern that has a high contrast of light and dark colours, or a very bright light. They occur because there is a slight time lag, after looking at a very strong image, before the eyes adjust to a new set of conditions. This activates the *rods* which are one of the two types of cells that make up the retina at the back of the eye. The rods register degrees of darkness. There are three sets of cones, one being sensitive to red wavelengths, one to blue, and one to green. Light of any colour which will be a mixture of wavelengths, activates the corresponding responsive cones. These retain a 'memory' of a colour for a few seconds after being exposed to it.

Various optical illusions are based on these effects. If you look at a set of black squares, and then try to concentrate on the white lines between them, you will see black spots where the white lines cross.

Why do parallel lines appear to meet in the distance?

We know that as things move further away from us, they appear to get smaller. This effect is known as the law of perspectives. Parallel lines going into the distance, like railway tracks, appear to draw together until they meet, and this is part of the same effect.

We use perspective to judge distances. Until about 1500, people in Europe did not fully understand perspective. In many early paintings it can be clearly seen that the different objects in them are often not the right size in relation to the distances between them.

Why does a curved mirror magnify?

There are two kinds of curved mirror. *Convex* mirrors curve or bulge out towards you. *Concave* mirrors curve inwards, away from you, like a cave.

Convex mirrors reflect objects from a wide area in front of them, but make them look smaller than life size.

Concave mirrors produce a magnified reflection of an object placed close in front. The reflection of an object further away is smaller, and also upsidedown.

To obtain a magnified image, the object must be placed nearer to the mirror than its focus. The focus of a mirror is the point at which parallel rays of light, such as sunrays, are brought to a focus. When an object is closer than the focus, the reflected rays *diverge*.

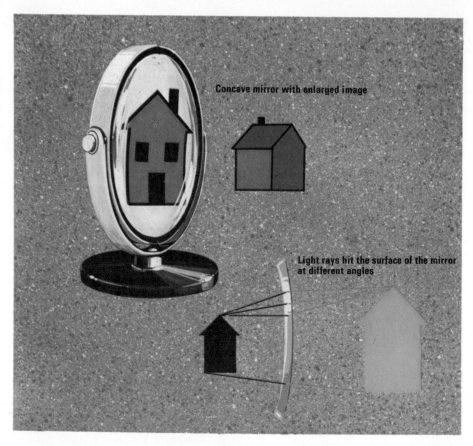

Concave mirror with enlarged image

Light rays hit the surface of the mirror at different angles

Why do mirrors invert?

All flat, or plane, mirrors obey the laws of reflection. The first law states that the reflected ray leaves the mirror at an angle equal to the angle at which the incident ray strikes it. These angles are measured between the incident and reflected rays and a line drawn perpendicular to the mirror. This particular line is called the *normal*.

The second law states that the incident ray, the reflected ray and the normal lie in the same plane. (This means that they could all be drawn on a flat piece of paper.)

The reflected ray leaves the mirror on the opposite side of the normal to the incident ray. Thus in its reflection, every point of an object appears on the opposite side of a central line. This is called mirror inversion or lateral inversion.

Why does a spoon in a glass of water look bent?

Light travels at different speeds through different materials. Its rate of travel is slowed down when it enters a more dense material.

At the surface between two materials, a ray of light changes its direction of travel. This is called *refraction*. As a ray passes into a more dense material it is bent, or refracted away from the surface. As it passes into a less dense material it is refracted towards the surface.

This is why a spoon standing partly immersed in a glass of water, looks as if it is bent at the water surface, when viewed from the side.

When viewed from above, refraction produces the effect of making water look shallower than it is. The eye sees an underwater object as if the light travelled from it to the eye in a straight line. In fact the light ray slopes down more steeply as it is refracted away from the surface. So the bottom is really further away than it appears.

What is a two-way mirror?

Two-way mirrors are popular with thriller writers. In their stories the mirrors are supposed to be used to spy on people who do not realize they are being watched. A two-way mirror looks like an ordinary mirror from one side, but you can look straight through it from the other side.

The mirror is only thinly coated with silver, on one side of the glass. Bright light is refracted through the glass and is scattered and reflected off the silver particles, producing a complete reflection on the illuminated side.

But some light passes straight through the glass. The result is that a person standing in darkness on the other side can see straight through, but he cannot be seen himself.

The same effect is produced by thick dust on a window, or sunglasses. If you look at a person wearing sunglasses, you see only your reflection in their lenses, but they can see you clearly.

Famous people who wish to travel about incognito, have smoked glass windows in their cars. This has the same result.

The person inside can see, but not be seen.

Apart from being used to produce theatrical effects, two-way mirrors have a use in optical instruments.

In the sextant, used by navigators, a half-silvered mirror is used to superimpose an image of the Sun on the instrument's scale. Using the laws of reflection, the altitude, or angle of declination of the Sun, can be measured. The ship's position can then be worked out, using a book of special tables.

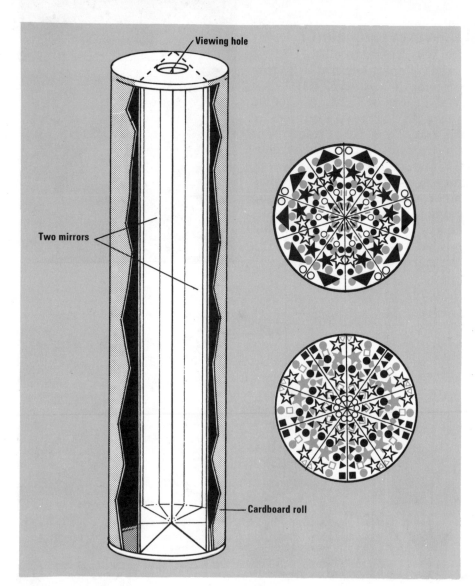

Viewing hole

Two mirrors

Cardboard roll

How does a kaleidoscope work?

A kaleidoscope is made of a tube with two mirrors in it. The mirrors are joined on one side so that they form a V down the length of the tube. Some kaleidoscopes make a pattern of what you see through the tube. Others usually have two pieces of clear material at the end you hold to the light. Pieces of different coloured plastic are fixed between them, to form the pattern.

When light enters the kaleidoscope it is bounced backwards and forwards by the mirrors so that your eye sees many images. One of these comes directly from the V made by the mirrors at the end of the kaleidoscope. All the others are reflected images of the V. The pieces of plastic in the V are therefore repeated several times, so that you see a circular pattern. To change the pattern, you simply shake the kaleidoscope.

Left: You could make your own kaleidoscope using cardboard for the outer tube and clear polythene for the material at the end that is held to the light.

How is mirror writing formed?

Ambulances often have mirror writing printed in large letters across the front. It takes a few seconds to work out what the words say; longer than it takes to read the right way round.

But the driver of a car in front of the ambulance can see the word from a glance in his rearview mirror, and quickly gets out of the way.

Mirror writing is the mirror image of normal writing. Each part of each letter is seen in the mirror exactly opposite itself.

How does a periscope work?

A simple periscope consists of two mirrors in a long tube, both tilted at 45 degrees to the viewing holes, but parallel to each other.

The tube is held upright, so that light from an object passes horizontally through the top hole and strikes the top mirror. It strikes the mirror at 45 degrees. The ray has thus been turned through a right angle of 90 degrees, from the horizontal to the perpendicular.

The light travels downwards to the second mirror which it also strikes at 45 degrees. So it is turned through another right angle to pass out of the viewing hole horizontally again.

The viewer sees a life-size, upright reflection of the object, as if it was at eye level. In fact, the object is as far above the viewer's head as the length of the periscope tube.

Periscopes are great fun to make for yourself and play with. They are well-known, too, for their use in submarines. A marine periscope is water-tight and highly mechanized. The tube can be rotated, so that all-round vision is possible. The periscope provides the crew with a view of what is happening above the surface, while the submarine cruises along beneath the waves.

What makes a rainbow?

If it is raining, and the Sun is also shining, turn your back on the Sun and look for a rainbow. Occasionally you may even see two rainbows; a second, fainter one curving outside the other.

The rainbow is a curved band with concentric strips of colour. From the outside of the bow inwards, the order of the colours is red, orange, yellow, green, blue, indigo (which cannot be distinguished separately) and violet. These are the colours of the spectrum. The rainbow is a huge spectrum, produced by the refraction of white light through the raindrops of water.

When a ray of light passes from a less dense to a more dense material, it is bent, or refracted, because light travels more slowly in the dense material. White light is a mixture of all the colours of the spectrum. Each colour has a different wavelength.

Shorter wavelengths are refracted or bent, more than the longer ones, because they have a higher frequency and travel faster. The different wavelengths become separated and we see the colours individually.

What is the spectrum?

The spectrum is the group of electromagnetic waves with wavelengths to which our eyes are sensitive. Each is registered by the brain as a different *colour*. The colours are red, orange, yellow, green, blue, indigo and violet. Colours at the red end of the spectrum have the longest wavelengths and at the lowest frequency. Those at the blue end have the shortest wavelengths and the highest frequency.

Radiation of wavelengths just longer than red light is known as infra-red. Radiation of wavelengths just shorter than violet is known as ultraviolet.

The normal white light that we see is a mixture of all the different wavelengths in the spectrum.

Added together, the colours produce the effect our brains register as white. If the white light is split up, so that we can see all the wavelengths separately, we can see the colours of the spectrum.

One way of doing this is to pass white light through a transparent substance which refracts or bends it, such as a glass prism. Radiation of different wavelengths travels at different speeds. The shorter the wavelength, the faster it travels. Consequently longer wavelengths are refracted through a smaller angle when they enter a new material, such as the glass prism. Each wavelength or colour passes out of the prism in a different place.

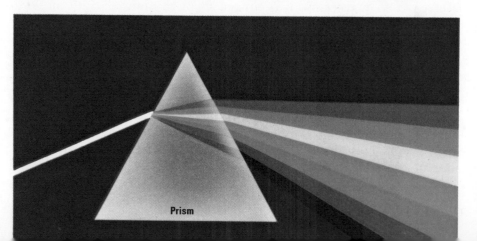

Prism

What are primary colours?

White light is a mixture of radiation at different wavelengths. Coloured light is radiation of a particular wavelength. As we have seen, if a beam of white light is split or refracted, it can be shown to contain all the colours of the spectrum.

But not all the colours of the spectrum are needed if we want to produce white light. It can be made by mixing the three *primary colours* as can be seen in the picture; there are red, green and blue. Any colour can be produced by mixing certain proportions of the primary colours together.

The colours of lights are altered by using colour filters. These block out certain wavelengths. This is because mixing colours in light is an *additive* process; different wavelengths are added together.

Mixing coloured paint is a quite different process. Once again, there are three primary colours. But these are red, yellow and blue. When all three are mixed together, they effectively produce black, or at least a very dark, muddy brown.

We see paint, and all normal solid objects, as having a colour because their surface *reflects* light of a particular wavelength. At the same time the surface absorbs

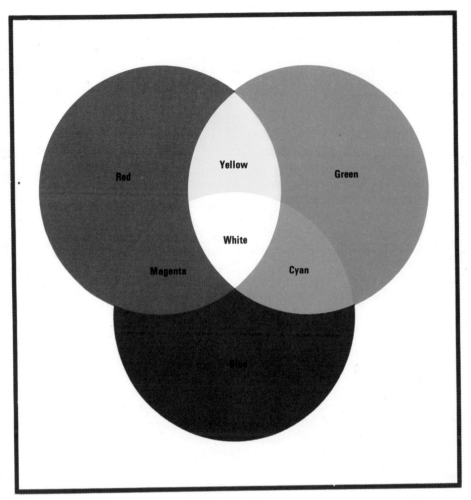

wavelengths of all the other colours.

When white light, which is a mixture of all wavelengths, falls on, say, a red object, all the wavelengths except that of red light are absorbed. Only red light is reflected in this case.

Each primary colour reflects only its particular wavelength; all others are absorbed. When all three primary colours are mixed together, all the wavelengths are absorbed, so the mixture appears black. Because mixing paint involves the absorption, or taking away of wavelengths, it is called a *subtractive* process.

What are complementary colours?

The three primary colours in coloured light are red, green and blue. Any colour can be obtained by mixing them in certain proportions. All three mixed together in equal proportions make white light.

When only two primary colours are mixed together they produce a *complementary colour*. Red and green mixed, produce *yellow*. Red and blue mixed produce a pinkish-purple colour called *magenta*. Blue and green mixed produce *cyan*, which is a greenish-blue peacock colour.

If the complementary colours are added together they produce white light. They are effectively another set of three primary colours.

In coloured paints or pigments, the three primary colours are red, yellow and blue.

Their corresponding complementary colours are orange, made from red and yellow, green made from blue and yellow, and purple made from red and blue.

In colour photography, a colour negative shows all the complementary colours to the real colours in the picture.

What is polaroid?

Polaroid is a commercially produced, transparent substance. It is used in many optical instruments such as camera filters and sun glasses. Polaroid is useful in these things because it cuts down glare from scattered or reflected light by polarizing the light.

Polaroid is the trade name for an important polarizing substance. It consists of thin sheets packed with minute crystals which are *doubly refracting*. These transmit *polarized light*.

Polarized light is light that has electrical vibrations in only one direction. Ordinary light rays contain vibrations in all directions perpendicular to the direction in which the ray is travelling.

To test for polaroid, two pieces of this special glass are needed. Hold one against the other, in front of a light source. Rotate one

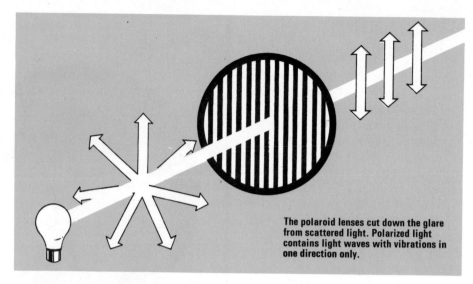

The polaroid lenses cut down the glare from scattered light. Polarized light contains light waves with vibrations in one direction only.

piece slowly. If both pieces are polaroid, the light will gradually be cut out, until no light is transmitted. This is because their two *planes of polarization* are at right angles to each other.

The first piece transmits light with vibrations in one plane only. The second cuts out all light, because it does not transmit any light with vibrations in that plane, and it is not receiving any to transmit in any other plane.

Continue to rotate the pieces and the light will reappear until they have been rotated through another 180°. Try this with two pairs of polaroid sunglasses.

Why is the sky blue?

The atmosphere is made up of a mixture of gases and minute dust particles. The gases are made up of tiny solid particles that are suspended in space.

When electromagnetic radiation in the form of white light travels through the atmosphere, it strikes some of these particles and is deflected in all directions. Some of the particles absorb the radiation and emit radiation of a shorter wavelength instead. The effect is known as scattering.

As a result, the light that reaches us contains more radiation with shorter wavelengths than longer wavelengths. So the blue colour of the shorter wavelengths predominates.

Seen from above the atmosphere, the sky appears black to pilots and astronauts, because there are no gas molecules in empty space to reflect any light.

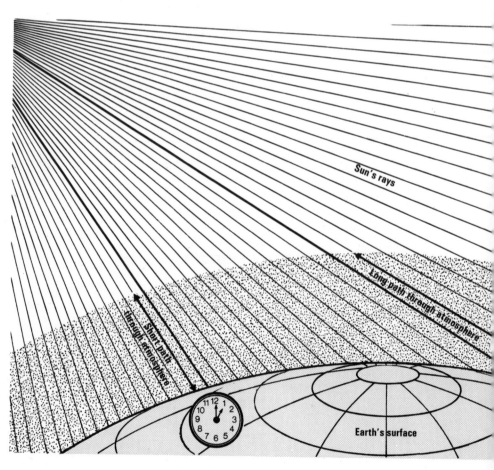

Sun's rays

Long path through atmosphere

Short path through atmosphere

Earth's surface

What is an X-ray?

X-rays are another form of electromagnetic radiation, just as light is, but they have a much shorter wavelength and a higher frequency light. They also possess very high energy. These properties enable X-rays to travel quite deep into solid matter, and in some cases, to pass right through. The lower the atomic weight and the lower the density of a material, the more transparent it is to X-rays. The degree of transparency and penetration can be detected photographically, because X-rays affect a photographic plate or film in a similar way to light radiation.

X-ray photographs have many uses in all sorts of work, from medicine to archaeology. In medicine, X-rays show up hard parts of the body and enable doctors to locate fractured bones, tumours and some other ailments.

X-rays are a form of ionizing radiation. That means that they possess enough energy to remove an electron from the structure of atoms in the molecules that they strike. Ionizing radiation is used in medicine to treat cancer by killing off the dangerously overactive cancer cells. The picture on the right shows an X-ray picture of somebody's chest.

X-rays are used in X-ray crystallography to examine the crystal structure of atoms and molecules. They are used in industry for nondestructive testing. By studying an X-ray photograph of a piece of equipment, engineers can detect faults in assembly, or flaws in the material, without dismantling it.

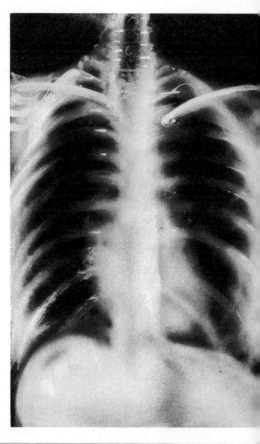

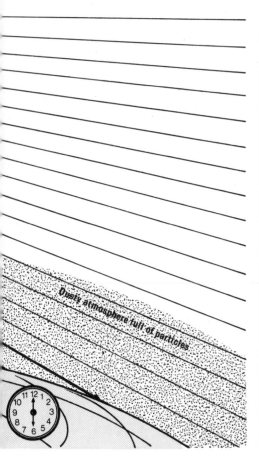

Dusty atmosphere full of particles

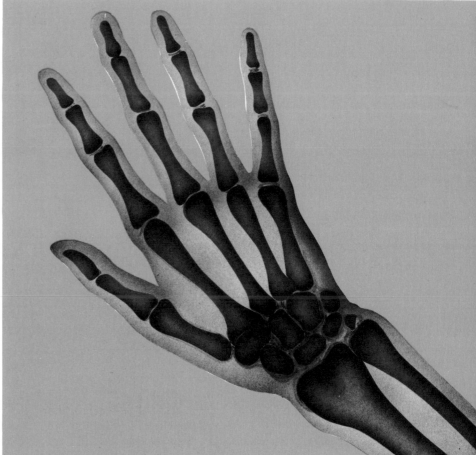

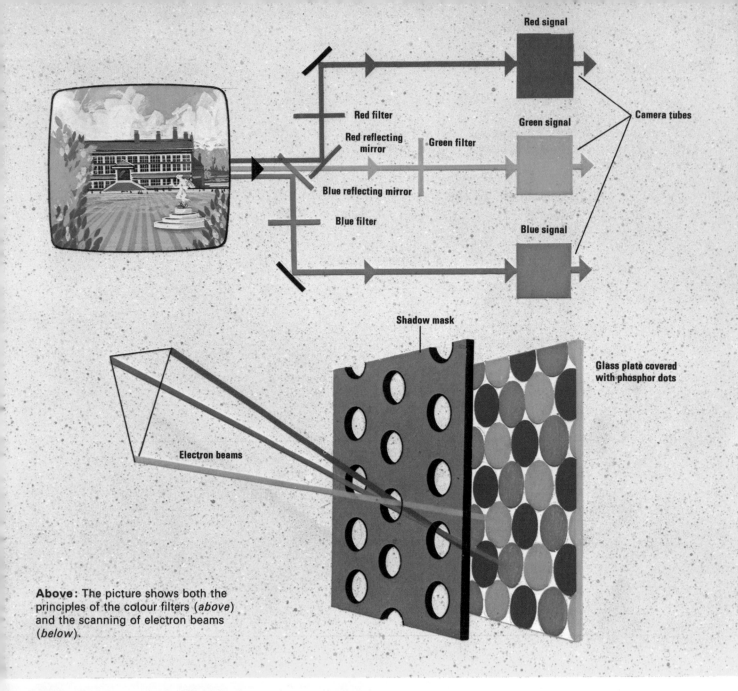

Red signal

Red filter

Red reflecting mirror

Green filter

Green signal

Camera tubes

Blue reflecting mirror

Blue filter

Blue signal

Shadow mask

Glass plate covered with phosphor dots

Electron beams

Above: The picture shows both the principles of the colour filters (*above*) and the scanning of electron beams (*below*).

How does colour TV work?

Colour television pictures are transmitted on three separate signals, as can be seen in the picture above. These are red, green and blue. In coloured light, all colour can be produced by adding together certain proportions of red, green and blue light, according to the laws of colour addition.

The colours are split by using mirrors and filters. The three coloured signals are then converted into electrical signals by

the camera tube so that they can be transmitted from the television transmitter.

The colour television receiver, or set, has a special screen, coated with tiny phosphor dots. These are arranged in clusters or groups of three.

Each one of the phosphor dots in a group emits a different primary colour when it receives a signal. Each cluster can therefore produce a mixture of red, green and blue. This varies according

to the signals received.

The television receiver receives the three separate signals from the transmitter and converts them into three scanning electron beams. These scan the screen at a fixed rate and excite the phosphor dots of the corresponding colour in each of the clusters.

Our eyes and brains finally see the combination of this array of dots as an image exactly like the scene being televized by the camera.

How do colour filters work?

Filters are made of transparent material which only allows light of a certain colour to pass through. This is the colour that the filter appears to be when looked at in white light. White light is made up of equal quantities of the three primary colours, red, green and blue. A yellow filter, for example, allows only red and green light to pass through. It filters out blue. Red and green light make yellow, so the beam of white light looks yellow when seen through the filter. A blue filter allows only blue light to pass through it and so on.

If a red light is shone through a green filter it produces a black beam, that is, no light at all. The green filter allows only green to pass through; as all red light is stopped, no light passes through at all.

Red filter   Yellow filter   Green filter

Why are sunsets red?

The sky overhead looks blue, especially when the Sun is high overhead. This is because there is more short-wave (blue) radiation in the light that reaches us, due to scattering by molecular particles in the upper atmosphere.

When the Sun is on the horizon the sky often appears orange or red because there is more long-wave (red) radiation in the light that reaches us. The short-wave (blue) light radiation has been lost because of collisions with dust particles in the lower atmosphere.

Light from the Sun on the horizon travels through the atmosphere close to the Earth's surface. When the Sun is overhead, the light has to travel a very much shorter distance through the atmosphere.

This part of the atmosphere is dense and laden with particles of dust and dirt. When light radiation strikes these particles it is absorbed and re-emitted at a longer wavelength. The longer the light's path through a dirt laden atmosphere, the greater the proportion of long-wave radiation in it.

Another factor is the frequency of the light radiation. The short-wave radiation waves vibrate at a much higher frequency than the long-wave radiation. This increases the chances of them striking a dust particle and being absorbed. If the light's path lies mainly through the lower atmosphere, much of the short-wave (blue) radiation is lost, so the sunset appears red.

The reddest sunsets are seen where the air is heavily polluted by smoke and fumes from industrial areas.

What is an electron microscope?

A microscope is an optical instrument used to produce an enlarged image of a minute object. This is done so that it can be studied in detail by the human eye.

In an ordinary microscope the object is illuminated by a beam of light and the image is then enlarged by means of glass lenses.

In an electron microscope, the object is bombarded by a stream of electrons, instead of a light beam. The electron stream is focused by means of magnetic lenses. These are powerful magnetic fields that can bend the electron beam and change its direction.

The image is focused onto a screen and is produced in a similar way to the image on a television screen.

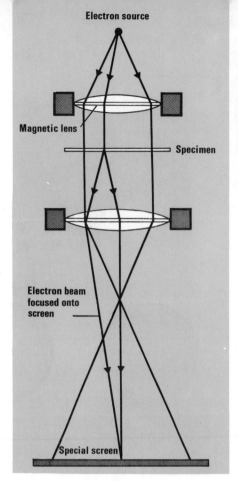

Electron source

Magnetic lens

Specimen

Electron beam focused onto screen

Special screen

Why do sodium lights sometimes glow red?

In some towns the street lights are an orangy-yellow colour. These are sodium vapour lamps. The light is produced by passing an electric current through sodium vapour at low pressure. The vapour molecules vibrate at a certain frequency and emit a yellow light.

When the lamp is switched on, the flow of electrons is slow at first, until all the vapour molecules become fully excited. While only a few of them are vibrating, at a low frequency, light of a longer wavelength is emitted. This is the pink or red colour that is sometimes seen when the street lighting first comes on, or when a lamp is not working properly.

Yellow sodium lights are used because the yellow light is not absorbed by fog or mist as much as white light is.

What does fluorescent mean?

A substance that is fluorescent is one that is capable of absorbing light of one wavelength, or colour and then re-emitting light of a different wavelength, or colour.

Road signs are sometimes made of fluorescent fabric or coated with fluorescent paint. They can then glow brightly when a light is shone on them.

Theatrical effects and decorations also make use of some fluorescent paints and materials.

Fluorescence is a form of luminescence; that is, the emission of light from an object which is not the result of the object being heated up.

A fluorescent lamp is one that consists of a glass tube thinly coated inside with a fluorescent substance. The tube contains a gas which emits ultra-violet (UV) light radiation when a voltage is applied to the lamp. The UV radiation is converted to visible light radiation by the fluorescent walls of the tube. This type of lighting is commonly known as strip lighting.

How do neon lights work?

Neon is a gas which glows when electricity is passed through it, if it is enclosed in a glass tube at a low pressure.

The tube contains two electrodes, the cathode and the anode, one at each end of the tube. An electric current is supplied to the lamp and the gas acts as a conductor between the two electrodes. The current is said to flow from the positive anode to the negative cathode. In fact there is an actual flow of electrons, which carry a negative charge, from the cathode to the anode.

The electrons are passed from atom to atom and during the exchange, light radiation is given off. This produces the intense coloured glow all along the tube.

Neon lights are used extensively in the brightly coloured illuminated signs that are used for street advertising at night.

Neon is one of the inert, or inactive gases that occurs naturally in the atmosphere in very small quantities. It is obtained by distilling liquid air.

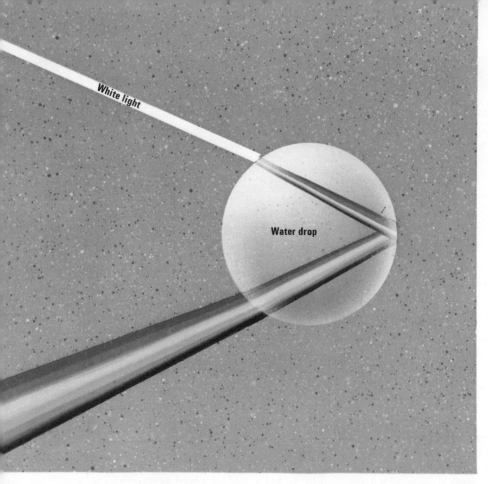

White light

Water drop

What makes rainbows in drops of water?

White light, such as sunlight, is made up of all the wavelengths in the visible spectrum. The shorter the wavelength, the higher the frequency of the vibrations; and the more vibrations there are, the more chances there are for collisions with the atoms of the substance they are travelling through.

The light rays are bent as soon as they strike a new substance, such as glass or water. The shorter wavelengths are bent more than the longer ones. Some of the rays are also reflected from the inside surface of a raindrop before they are refracted again as they pass out of it. Different wavelengths leave the raindrop at different points and these are seen as the separate colours of the rainbow.

What makes rainbows in bubbles?

In soap bubbles, the rainbow effect is produced by the phenomenon known as *interference*. The thin, filmy wall of a soap bubble is in fact only a few molecules thick.

Very thin films cause light waves of certain wavelengths to be cancelled out. The colour that is cancelled out depends on the wavelength of that colour in relation to the thickness of the film.

Where a colour has been cancelled out of a beam of white light, its complementary colour is seen. This gives the soap bubble its colour. The colour will change as the film changes in thickness, usually by evaporating until the bubble bursts. Different colours will be seen on different parts of the bubble because the soap film is of varying thickness.

What makes the coloured rings on puddles?

The coloured rings on puddles are usually caused by a thin film of oil spread over the surface. Different colours are seen where the oil film is of different thickness.

Thin films produce coloured, rainbow effects because of the interference of light waves. Light travels in waves which have crests and troughs just like those in water. When two waves cross each other, where the crest of one meets the trough of another, their effect is zero.

In water waves, this means the water is flat at that particular point. In light waves, it means that wavelengths are cancelled out of the light beam. The light beam then takes on the complementary colour to the colour of the wavelength cancelled out.

What are moiré patterns?

A moiré pattern is the effect produced when light shines through two gratings which are moving over each other. The gratings could be formed by two pieces of net curtain moving in the wind, or two sets of railings which are stationary, but appear to move as you walk or travel past, or two pieces of gauze which you can move separately. All sorts of patterns appear in different shapes. They may produce a series of wavy lines, or rings.

Moiré patterns have always been particularly popular for the effect they produce in water silks.

Moiré patterns are caused by the interference of trains of light waves. Interference occurs when separate trains of light travel to your eye along paths which are slightly different in length. Some of the trains of light waves cancel each other out.

What is a decibel?

A decibel is the unit of measurement which we normally use to measure the intensity or loudness of sound. A sound of zero decibels is just too faint for the human ear to hear. A whisper makes a noise of about 20 decibels, ordinary conversation about 50, heavy traffic about 90 and an aircraft 100 to 200 decibels. Any sudden noise above 140 decibels is very dangerous to the unprotected ear.

How do we hear sounds?

Sounds are caused by the varying vibrations of air molecules.

Sound waves would look like corn moving in the wind if you could see them. When stalks of corn are blown over slightly you see wave movements travelling across the field.

In the same way, sound waves cause each air molecule to bump its neighbour, which in turn bumps its neighbour. In this way, the molecules crowd against each other, causing a very slight increase in pressure. They then move back, causing the pressure to fall once again.

The flap of the outer ear is a funnel which collects the sound waves as they reach your ear, then passing along a short tube to the ear drum. The changes of pressure in the sound wave make the drum vibrate. This causes a tiny bone called the hammer, which touches the drum, to vibrate in its turn.

The hammer's vibrations then pass through two more small bones called the anvil and the stirrup. They finally reach a shell-shaped organ called the cochlea. It is here that the vibrations are converted into electrical messages. Finally, these are carried by nerves to the brain.

SOUND	DECIBELS	LOUDNESS
Saturn rocket at take off	200	Dangerously loud
Aircraft engine	100–200	Painfully loud
Pneumatic drill	100	Very loud
Heavy traffic	90	Very loud
Record player	70	Loud
Ordinary conversation	40–60	Moderate
Quiet home	30	Faint
Whisper	20	Very faint
Rustling of leaves on a tree	10	Very faint

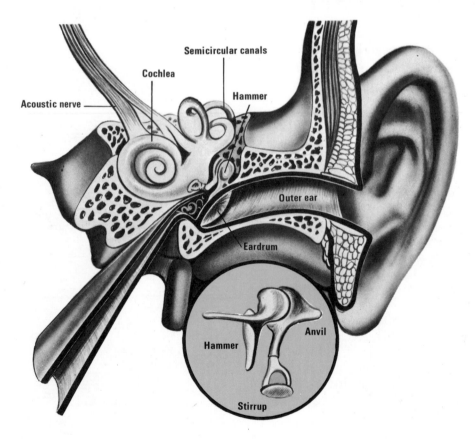

What is the sound barrier?

The sound barrier is the imaginary barrier through which a plane passes when it reaches the speed of sound. This is a speed of approximately 332 metres per second, or 760 m.p.h. at sea level. But it is lower in the thinner air at high altitudes.

As the aircraft flies, it creates waves in the air, just as the prow of a ship creates a bow wave. As the speed of the aircraft increases, the waves are pushed closer and closer together. When the aircraft reaches the speed of sound, the pressure waves are violently disturbed and turn into a sound wave. This travels to the ground and is heard as a tremendously loud bang, known as the *sonic boom*.

Flight at a speed less than the speed of sound is known as subsonic flight. Flight at speeds greater than the speed of sound is known as supersonic flight.

There is great controversy about the use of supersonic aircraft. This is because the sonic bangs they create are so disturbing. It is one of the forms of pollution that are rapidly becoming an unpleasantly familiar part of our way of life. Sudden, loud noises are a danger to the mental and physical health of both men and animals.

The recently developed Anglo-French supersonic passenger aircraft, *Concorde*, was severely criticised for the amount of noise it made. It had a cruising speed of 2320 k.p.h., which is almost twice the speed of sound.

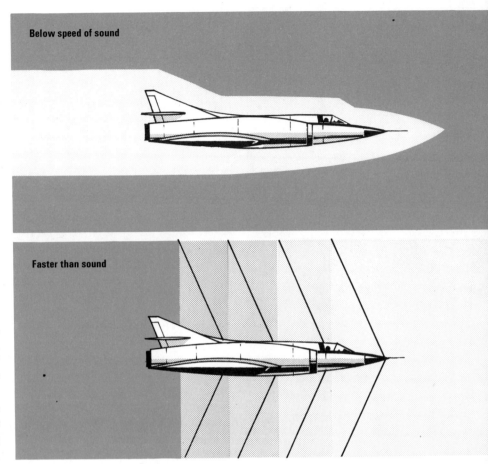

Below speed of sound

Faster than sound

What is an echo?

Sounds are reflected off large surfaces, rather like light off a mirror, but more slowly.

One blow of a hammer in a large, empty room will be heard several times. It is first heard as the actual sound of the blow reaches your ear, and afterwards, as a series of echoes. The echoes are the result of the sound waves travelling across the room. They are reflected off the wall, travel back and are reflected again, several times until the sound dies away.

You can hear echoes in large empty places where there are high walls, such as in empty rooms, long corridors, tunnels, caves or deep mountain valleys. There are few objects to absorb the sound and large, flat surfaces to reflect it.

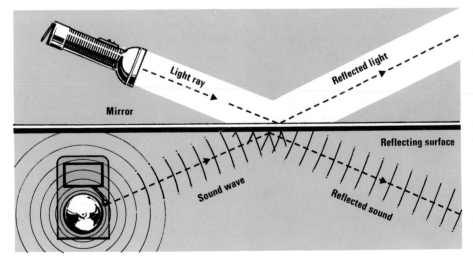

Light ray · Reflected light · Mirror · Reflecting surface · Sound wave · Reflected sound

Why does thunder follow lightning?

The sound of lightning travels at a speed of $\frac{1}{3}$ kilometre per second. The light reaches us almost instantaneously. To work out how far away the heart of a storm is, count the number of seconds between the flash and the crash. Then divide by three to work out its distance in kilometres. As the storm travels nearer, the time between the two will grow less.

Lightning is caused by an electric discharge across air molecules. The atmospheric conditions cause parts of the clouds to become positively charged, air molecules in another part to become positively charged and air molecules in yet another part to become negatively charged. When a potential difference builds up, a current flashes from the positive to the negative part of the cloud. In fact, there are up to ten flashes along the same path, in quick succession. The eye sees them as one continuous streak.

The current heats the air up and causes it to expand. Because there are several strokes in quick succession, the rapid expansion and contraction of the air causes huge sound waves to build up. These produce the thunderclap.

The electrical discharge can take place from cloud to cloud, or from a cloud to the ground. A tree or high building which is struck by lightning can be badly burnt. To safeguard against this, high buildings have lightning conductors. These are conductors with an insulated casing that project above the highest point of the building, such as the tip of a church spire. The lightning strikes the conductor and is conducted safely down the side of the building into the earth.

How does radar work?

Radar is an abbreviation of the name for RAdio Detecting And Ranging systems.

A radar aerial is dish-shaped. It transmits short-wave radio signals that are reflected off objects in their path and travel back to the aerial which also acts as a receiver. The incoming signal is passed to a cathode-ray tube so that it can be seen on a screen like a television screen.

As the direction of the signal and the time it takes to travel to the object and back can both be measured, the exact position of the object can be calculated.

The strength of the returning signal indicates what type of material it has been reflected off. The metal in vehicles produces a much stronger signal than the dense cloud at the centre of a hurricane, for example.

What makes some music loud?

The loudness, or volume, of a sound depends on the amount of energy that goes into making the sound.

The sound is produced by the vibration of air molecules. The rate at which the molecules vibrate determines the pitch of the sound, that is, whether it sounds high or low. The amplitude of the vibrations determines the volume or loudness of the sound. The amplitude of the vibration is the height, or depth of a wave.

The molecules use up energy as they vibrate. Sound waves therefore tend to decrease in amplitude and the sound grows quieter and dies away, unless more energy is supplied.

In many musical instruments, the energy is supplied by human muscles. They may be used to pluck a string, blow into a pipe or strike a drum, for example.

The loudest sounds are produced by the greatest movement of the air. This can be seen in a roll of drums, plucking, striking or bowing a string very hard, or blowing a lot of air into a pipe.

When sound is reproduced by electrical means, such as in radio, the volume can be increased by an amplifier. This is an electronic device that increases the amplitude of the sound output by putting in more energy. The extra energy is drawn from a power supply. Amplifiers are used with electric guitars.

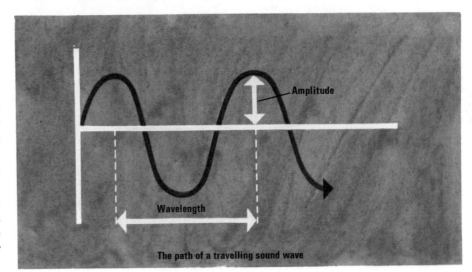

Amplitude

Wavelength

The path of a travelling sound wave

What is radar used for?

Radar is used for navigation and tracking systems. Ships and aircraft can locate their positions by directing a radar beam at known points on land. They can also avoid collision courses by keeping track of other moving vehicles.

Radar tracking systems keep a check on the movements of all aircraft or ships within their range. They are also used for missile detection.

Automatic control systems for guiding vehicles and missiles have been developed. This involves feeding the incoming signal into a computer.

Radar is useful for studying weather conditions and is invaluable for overcoming them. Unlike all tracking and navigation by sight, radar is unaffected by darkness, fog or clouds.

The 250-foot radio telescope at Jodrell Bank

99

How does a recorder make music?

A recorder is a wind instrument consisting of a pipe with an open end. At specific intervals along the pipe there are holes. These can be closed by covering them with the fingers.

When the column of air inside the pipe vibrates, it produces a musical note. It can be made to vibrate by blowing through the mouthpiece. As the air passes the sharp edge of the opening in front of the mouthpiece, it sets up eddies. These pass down the pipe in waves.

The length of the air column is varied by placing the fingers over the holes in the stem. The shorter the air column, the more vibrations the air makes.

How does a guitar make music?

A guitar is a stringed instrument. It produces a musical sound when the strings are plucked. This sets up vibrations in the strings, which are stretched across an opening in the hollow body of the guitar. The vibrations in the strings cause the air inside the guitar to vibrate or *resonate*.

The note produced by a string depends on its tautness and its length.

The strings can be wound tighter before playing to produce higher notes while playing. The effective length of a string is reduced by pressing down onto one of the metal ridges, or frets, on the neck. This also produces a higher note.

How do we get a sound from a record disc?

The surface of a record has a continuous spiral groove in it, leading from the edge to the centre. In the groove are minute waves and bumps, which cause the needle travelling along it to vibrate. These vibrations are converted into a variable electric current by a small component in the pick-up known as the cartridge. The current passes to the amplifier, which magnifies it many times. This amplified current is then fed to the speaker.

The speaker consists of an electromagnet and a cone. In this the electrical energy of the current is converted into mechanical energy, making the cone vibrate. The vibrations set up sound waves and the listener hears a reproduction of the sound that was originally recorded on the record.

You can tell which parts of a record will sound loud and which will be quieter, by looking carefully at the disc. The quiet passages are those where the grooves are very fine and closely spaced. The loud passages are where the grooves are wider apart.

Below: This picture shows how a record is made from the time when the music is first recorded, to the finished product on the record player.

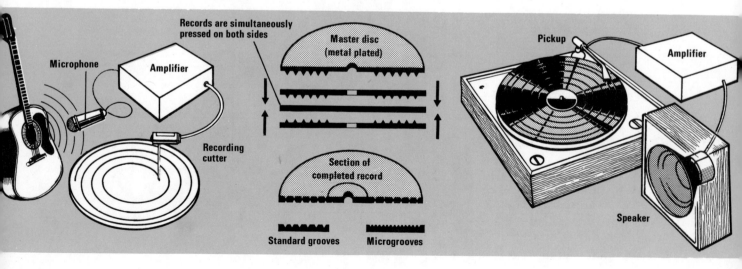

Microphone   Amplifier   Records are simultaneously pressed on both sides   Master disc (metal plated)   Pickup   Amplifier

Recording cutter   Section of completed record   Speaker

Standard grooves   Microgrooves

What is quadrophonic sound?

At a live performance of music, the sound travels to you from all the individual players and singers in their different positions. If you play a record on an ordinary record player, all the sound comes to you from one speaker, so you hear it as if it all came from a single point.

Quadrophonic sound is an attempt to reproduce the sounds you hear from all directions at a live performance. In the mid-1950s, stereophonic sound equipment was marketed. This system involves two speakers which reproduce the sound as if it came from a position on a straight line drawn between the two speakers. Stereophonic sound is more realistic than sound from one speaker, because the sound is heard as if it was coming from the correct position, from left to right, in front of the listener.

Quadrophonic sound is an improvement on stereophonic sound in two ways. It adds depth, so that the players are heard as if they were positioned before or behind each other. It also reproduces the sound which would be reflected off the side and back walls, as it would be at a live performance.

To produce these effects, four speakers are used, two placed in front of the listener, and two behind him. But it cannot be produced from an ordinary record just by using four speakers. A stereophonic record is specially made to send different sounds to the two speakers and with a quadrophonic record a slightly different sound is sent to each of the four speakers. A special amplifier is also needed to select and distribute the signals picked up from the record.

Right: The top picture represents stereophonic sound. Quadrophonic sound is shown below with the sound waves coming from four speakers.

101

How does a telephone work?

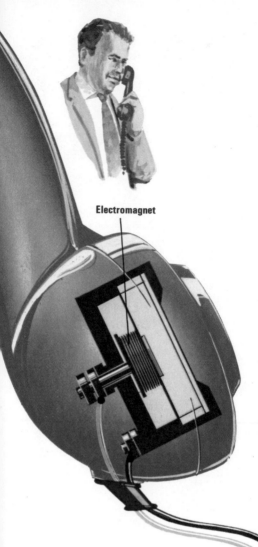

Electromagnet

A telephone converts sounds into electric currents, so that they can be transmitted to a place that is out of normal hearing range. A second instrument receives the current and reconverts it to the original audible sounds. The telephone was invented by Alexander Graham Bell in 1876.

Each telephone handset contains an earphone receiver and a microphone transmitter. In both of these, there is a movable diaphragm and an electromagnet.

In the transmitter, the sound waves produced by the speaker's voice cause the diaphragm to vibrate. This movement produces changes in the strength of the magnetism of the electromagnet behind it. The magnetism of varying strength produces a correspondingly variable electric current.

At the receiver, another electromagnet uses the varying current to reproduce movements in the receiver diaphragm. These are exactly the same as those produced in the first diaphragm by the voice. These movements in the receiver diaphragm produce the sound waves heard by the listener, who hears an almost perfect reproduction of the speaker's voice.

Telephones are connected to telephone exchanges by wires, where they can be linked to another telephone through the switching mechanism. The exchange may be manual, where the operator has to plug the call into the socket with the right number, or they can be automatic, where relays select the position mechanically.

For long distance calls the current is amplified. This can be relayed along co-axial cables. As many as 3600 calls can be relayed along the same cable at the same time and are sorted out, electronically, at the other end.

Why does a magnet pick up a string of pins?

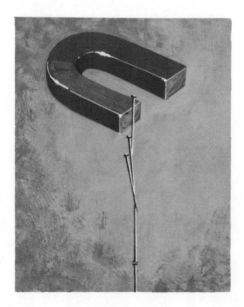

Dip a magnet into a pile of loose pins and it will come out bristling with them; some of them sticking to the magnet, some sticking to other pins.

The magnet exerts a force over the space around it which is known as the *magnetic field*. The way in which the space is magnetized follows a definite pattern, dependent on the shape of the magnet. This pattern can be represented by a series of lines, known as *lines of force*. When a metal object is placed near a magnet, these lines of force flow into it, turning the object into a weaker magnet that can attract other objects.

This is what happens to the chain of pins. Each pin becomes a very small, individual magnet itself, attracting another pin. The pins are not permanent magnets. When the main magnet is removed, the chain collapses as lines of magnetic force no longer flow through the pins.

Metal diaphragm

How can you magnetize something?

The simplest way to magnetize a piece of iron, such as a nail, is to stroke it with another magnet. Use the end of a bar magnet, holding it like a pencil. Stroke the nail firmly, making each stroke in the same direction and keeping the magnet well away from the nail when returning it to the beginning.

After a few strokes, the nail should have become a strong enough magnet to attract other pieces of metal.

Another way to magnetize the nail is to wrap a coil of wire around it, laying the coils along its length. Attach the ends of the wire to a battery. After a current has passed through the wire, the nail will be magnetized.

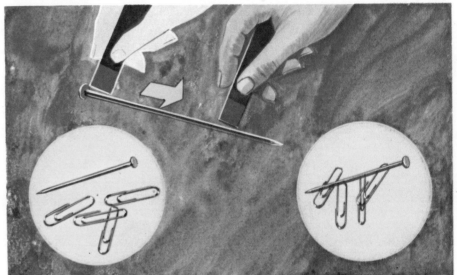

How can you tell if a piece of metal is a magnet?

Two nails will be attracted and stick together if one of them has been magnetized. They may also stick together if they are both magnetized, and the north pole of one is brought up to the south pole of the other. However, if two north poles or two south poles are brought together, they will repel each other because *like* poles of the same sign (north or south) always repel each other. *Unlike* poles of the opposite sign always attract each other. These are two of the basic laws of magnetism. Repulsion is necessary to prove that a piece of metal is a magnet.

Every particle in a nail is like a miniature bar magnet. Before it is magnetized these lie at random in all directions and their total magnetic effect is zero because they cancel each other out.

Stroking the piece of iron with the pole of a magnet attracts all the poles of opposite sign in the particles. The *orientation* of their magnetism is changed, so that they all lie in the same direction, producing a north pole at one end of the piece of iron, and a south pole at the other.

An electric current passed through a coil which is also wrapped around a piece of iron also brings the magnetism of all the particles into alignment.

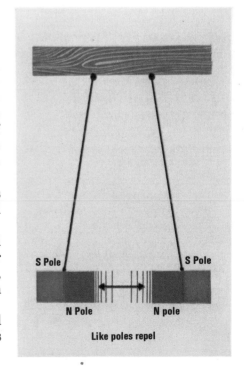

S Pole   S Pole

N Pole   N pole

Like poles repel

Where does electricity come from?

Electricity is vital to our modern way of life. We need it for lighting, heating, cooking, air-conditioning, refrigeration, transport, machinery, entertainment and communications. Without it we could certainly not live our lives in the way most of us do today.

Electricity exists in many forms. It can be transformed into light in a light bulb, heat in an electric fire, or sound in a telephone.

Where does electricity come from in the first place? We receive it in our homes down wires, from the power transmission lines. It has come from the power station where it was generated and changed to a suitable voltage by transformers.

The electricity is generated by means of electromagnetic induction. Huge electromagnets are rotated inside coils of wire. This induces a current in the wire. The power to rotate the generator is obtained from turbines operated by steam power. This in turn is obtained from burning coal, or from a nuclear reactor, or from water power in a hydroelectric power station.

Electricity also reaches our homes in the form of electromagnetic waves. They are picked up by an aerial and converted into sound on a radio, or a picture on a television screen.

Electricity occurs in nature in the form of lightning and also in the electrical discharge that causes the phenomenon known as St Elmo's fire. This is the ghostly halo seen around the tips of ships' masts and aircrafts' wings during storms.

Another form of natural electricity is static electricity. It causes a piece of amber which has been rubbed hard, to attract small pieces of fluff or paper. Nowa-days, it is more common to see it shown by a gramophone record attracting dust and fluff. It was, in fact, the ancient Greeks who gave electricity the name *elektron*, which is the Greek name for amber. The records of the Greek philosopher Thales who lived about 600 B.C. show that he carried out such experiments with amber.

Electricity can be produced chemically by the process known as electrolysis.

Small electric currents are also produced by the interaction of certain metals when they are both heated. This is known as thermoelectricity.

All electricity is associated with the movement of electrons, which exist in every atom of matter. These electrons carry an electric charge and it is the flow of electrons which produces an electric current.

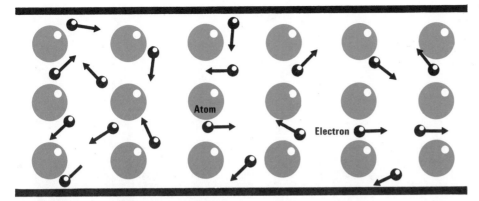

When electrons move at random there is no current

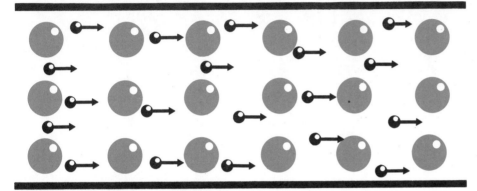

When electrons move in the same direction the current flows

What is an electric current?

An electric current is a flow of electrons through a conductor.

An electron is a part of an atom. All atoms consist of a central part, or nucleus, which has a positive charge, and one or more electrons. These are tiny, negatively charged particles that travel in orbit round the nucleus like planets round a sun.

Each element has a different number of electrons in its atoms. Some elements have electrons that are free to move from atom to atom. Many of these are metals. Normally, the electrons are moving about among the atoms in all directions at random. But the electrons can all be made to flow in the same direction. This continuous flow of electrons is called an electric current.

Electric current is measured in units called *amps*.

Who discovered how to make electricity?

A famous English physicist and chemist, Michael Faraday, who was born in 1791, made many important discoveries concerning electricity, magnetism and electrolysis. These included his experiments in which he found that, if a wire moves through a magnetic field, a current is induced in the wire. This is called *electromagnetic induction*. In fact, Faraday used a stationary coil of wire, known as a solenoid. He attached this to a galvanometer, which indicated that a current flowed in the wire when a magnet was moved in and out of the solenoid. The direction in which the current flowed depended on which way the magnet was moving.

This discovery led to the development of the generator.

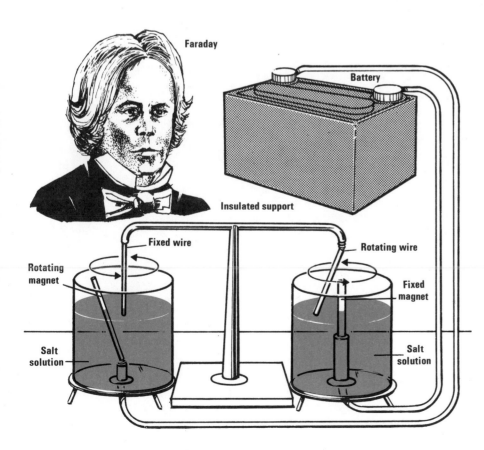

Faraday

Battery

Insulated support

Rotating magnet

Fixed wire

Rotating wire

Fixed magnet

Salt solution

Salt solution

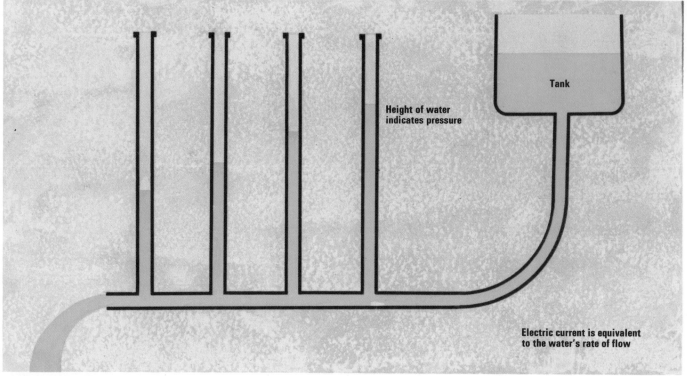

Tank

Height of water indicates pressure

Electric current is equivalent to the water's rate of flow

What is voltage?

Voltage is a measure of potential difference.

The size or strength of the potential difference that will cause a current to flow through a conductor is measured in *volts*.

The unit is named after the Italian scientist, Count Alessandro Volta, who lived from 1745 to 1827. He studied electricity and built the first battery, or *voltaic pile*. This provided a source of *electromotive force* (e.m.f.) or potential, that could be used to make a current flow through a conductor.

One volt is defined as the potential difference that exists between two points in a conductor that is carrying a current of one amp and using one watt of power.

Voltage is measured with an instrument known as a voltmeter. It contains a very high resistance so that the current continues to flow mainly through the conductor across which the voltage is to be measured.

Voltage can be increased or decreased by *transformers*.

Throughout the U.K. electricity is transmitted on power lines, in which the voltage may be as high as 400,000 volts. Very high voltages are dangerous and the power lines have to be very well insulated. To be used in homes, the voltage has to be reduced by transformers to about 240 volts.

What is potential difference?

An electric current flows through a conductor because there is a *potential difference* between the two ends. If you compare the electric current to water flowing along a pipe, the potential difference is equivalent to the difference in water pressure at the ends of the pipe. The water will only flow when there is a difference in pressure between the two ends of the pipe. And the greater the pressure, the more swiftly it will flow. The current is equivalent to the water's rate of flow.

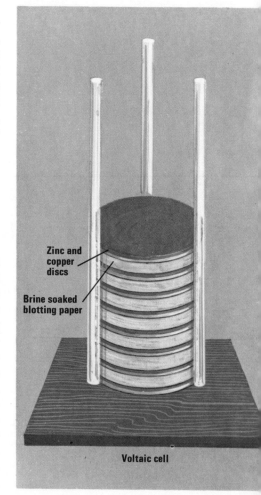

Zinc and copper discs

Brine soaked blotting paper

Voltaic cell

106

How is electricity measured?

All modern homes use power supplied by the mains electricity supply. The amount that is used is measured by a meter (a picture of one is shown on the right). This contains a digital counter or clock, showing the number of units that have been consumed.

The units are kilowatt-hours. The meter registers how many kilowatts of power have been used up each hour.

The watt is the unit of power which is named after Sir James Watt. One watt is the amount of power, or energy, used per second, when a current of one amp flows through a conductor which has a potential difference of one volt across it.

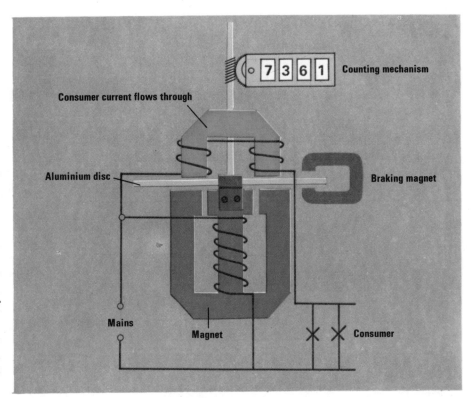

Counting mechanism

Consumer current flows through

Aluminium disc

Braking magnet

Mains

Magnet

Consumer

What are fuses for?

Fuses are intended to make an electric circuit safe from the danger of overheating. If the current does rise towards danger level, it causes heating in the thin fuse wire. This will melt, breaking the circuit and stopping the current from flowing.

What causes electric shocks?

A person may receive an electric shock if he touches a badly insulated, *live* electrical appliance; that is, an appliance that has a voltage across it.

If the appliance is at a positive potential a current will try to flow through the body to a place at a lower potential, such as the earth, or a metal object. A person wearing rubber boots is safer than one without, because with them he is insulated from the ground. This means that he does not provide a conducting path for the electricity. But if he touches say, a car battery terminal while he holds onto the metal bodywork of the car with his other hand, he will receive a shock from the battery.

People receive shocks from appliances plugged into the mains if the insulation on them breaks down. Handheld appliances usually have rubber or plastic covered handles, as do many tools such as screwdrivers and pliers intended for touching electrical fittings.

107

What does a battery do?

A battery is a set of voltaic cells that is used to supply a voltage to a circuit.

Ordinary dry batteries are made of a type of Leclanché cell. They consist of a zinc case containing a carbon rod with a brass cap. The rod is surrounded by powdered manganese dioxide and the rest of the case is filled with ammonium chloride paste.

The base of the zinc case and the brass cap are the two connection points. When the battery is connected into a circuit a chemical reaction takes place inside the battery. This produces a potential difference across the terminals that causes a current to flow through the circuit.

A dry battery, or primary cell, produces about 1·5 volts. This is sufficient to light a small torch.

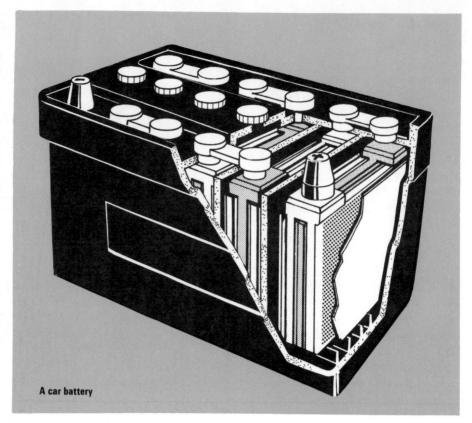

A car battery

How does a car battery keep going?

A car battery is a secondary cell, also called an *accumulator*.

Unlike the dry battery, the chemicals in an accumulator are not used up. Instead they are simply changed.

In the car battery, each of the six cells contains two lead plates. These are the electrodes and they are immersed in an electrolyte, a solution of sulphuric acid.

The cells are connected in series so that they put out twelve volts from the large terminals at each side to which heavy leads are attached.

When the battery is discharging, current is drawn from it to work the lights and drive the starter motor, indicators, horn and so on. In the chemical change that takes place, lead sulphate is deposited on the plates and the acid becomes less concentrated.

The battery is recharged by passing a current through it in the opposite direction. This current is produced by the dynamo, which is turned by the car engine. During recharging, the acid becomes more concentrated and the lead plates change back.

Below: The two diagrams show a car battery, first as it is charging and then as it is discharging. To charge the battery a current is produced by the dynamo which is turned by the engine.

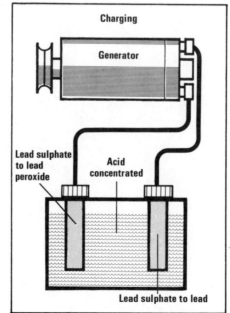

Charging

Generator

Lead sulphate to lead peroxide

Acid concentrated

Lead sulphate to lead

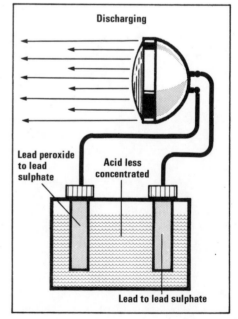

Discharging

Lead peroxide to lead sulphate

Acid less concentrated

Lead to lead sulphate

How does a bicycle dynamo work?

Lights for a bicycle can be powered either by dry batteries or by a simple dynamo, which works by electromagnetic induction.

The dynamo consists of a permanent magnet that is rotated inside a coil. The magnet is connected to a small drive wheel which rests against the back wheel rim of the bicycle. As the cycle wheel rotates, it causes the dynamo drive wheel to turn. As the permanent magnet rotates it induces an electric current in the coil.

The lamps are connected to the coil and are lit by the induced current. The lamps are dim at first but grow brighter as the cyclist builds up speed.

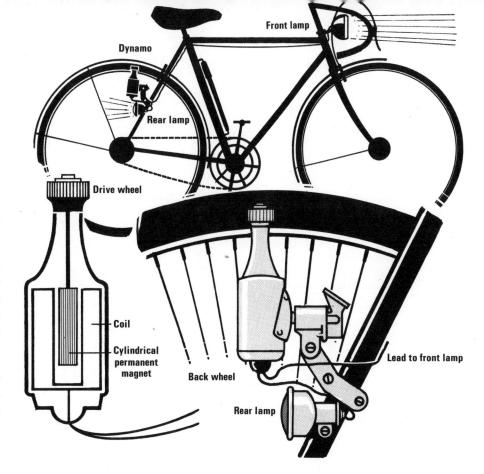

What is an electromagnet?

When a piece of wire is wound into a long coil and a current is passed through it, the coil behaves like a magnet (*see page* 103). It will deflect a compass needle. In fact, any conductor carrying a current has a magnetic field. If the direction of the current is changed, so is the magnetic field.

The strength of the magnetism in the coils can be increased by pushing a piece of soft iron down its centre. As soon as a current is passed through the coil, the iron is magnetized. When the current is switched off, it soon loses its magnetism.

A magnet that is produced by an electromagnetic effect is called an electromagnet.

Electromagnets have many uses where a strong but temporary magnet is needed. They are used in electric bells with a make-and-break circuit. In this, the circuit is closed by pressing the bell. This causes a current to flow through the coils of an electromagnet. This magnet attracts a flexible metal strip that breaks the circuit. The current ceases and the electromagnet stops attracting the strip. Then it falls back, closes the circuit and the electromagnet attracts it again. The continuous movement of the strip vibrates the arm of the hammer against the bell.

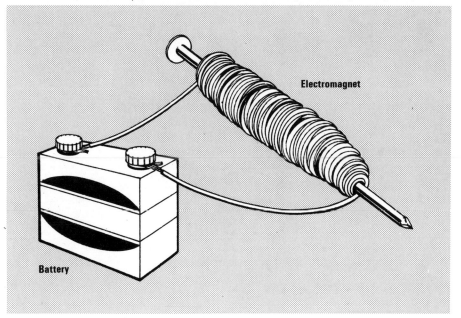

What is a transformer?

If a magnet is moved through a coil or wire, it can produce a current in the wire. This is called *electromagnetic induction*. Transformers work by electromagnetic induction.

They contain a soft iron core which is wrapped with a few turns of wire that form the *primary coil*. An alternating current flows through this wire. The core is also wrapped with a *secondary coil* of wire that has a different number of turns. If the secondary coil contains more turns than the primary coil, it will have a greater output voltage than that of the primary input. The current in the secondary coil is induced by the constantly fluctuating magnetism of the soft iron core, induced by the alternating current in the primary coil.

The ratio of input to output voltages is roughly equal to the ratio of the number of turns of wire in the primary and secondary coils.

A transformer that changes current at one voltage to current at a higher voltage is called a step-up transformer. One that changes the voltage down is called a step-down transformer.

Step-down transformers are used to reduce the voltage of 400,000 volts, at which the mains supply is transmitted across the country, to the voltage at which it is used in our homes, about 240 volts.

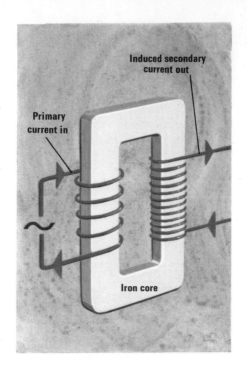

What is a generator?

A generator is a machine that uses mechanical energy to produce electrical energy. Small generators are also called dynamos. The principle they work on is that of electromagnetic induction.

If a permanent magnet is moved in and out of a coil of wire, it induces, or generates an electric current in the wire. Conversely, if a coil of wire is rotated in a magnetic field, a current is induced in the wire.

The magnetic field around a magnet is made up of invisible lines of force which are rather similar to the ridges in a ploughed field. The pattern these lines make up depends on the shape of the magnet. When a coil is rotated in a magnetic field, it cuts across the invisible lines of force. The faster these lines are cut by the coil, the greater the current induced in it. The number of turns of wire in the coil also affects the size of the current; the more turns there are, the greater the current.

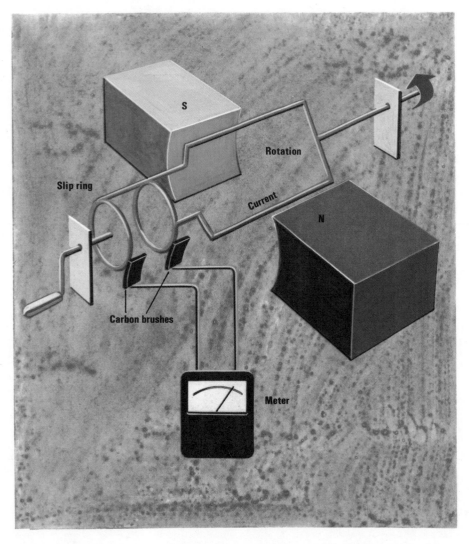

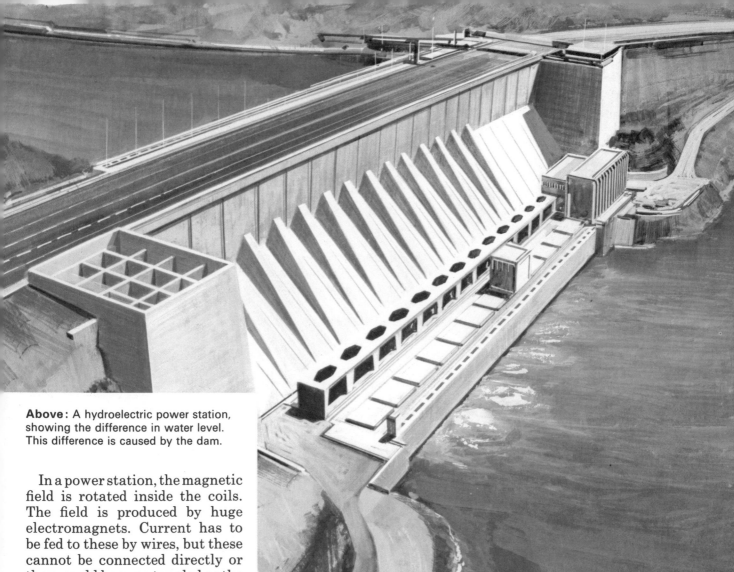

Above: A hydroelectric power station, showing the difference in water level. This difference is caused by the dam.

In a power station, the magnetic field is rotated inside the coils. The field is produced by huge electromagnets. Current has to be fed to these by wires, but these cannot be connected directly or they would become tangled as the electromagnet rotated. The electrical connection is made by slip rings and carbon brushes. The brushes are fixed, and slide over the rotating slip rings, so that there is a permanent conducting path.

Mechanical energy is used to turn the electromagnets and it may be produced by a variety of means. In *turbo-generators* the shaft is rotated by a huge turbine. The turbine is rotated by water in a hydroelectric power station, or by steam produced by burning coal, oil or nuclear fuel.

Electric generators are vital to our way of life. They provide the power we use for transport, heating, lighting, factory machinery and all the electrical appliances we use in our homes every day.

What is hydroelectricity?

Hydroelectricity is electrical power obtained as a result of using water-power to drive a dynamo.

A dynamo converts mechanical energy into electrical energy. The mechanical energy provides the turning force required to rotate the armature, or rotor coil in the field of the electromagnet. This induces an alternating current, that is, one that builds up, then drops back to zero, builds up in the opposite direction and returns to zero, in a continuous cycle. The mechanical energy provides the turning force required to rotate the shaft in the generator.

In the case of a hydroelectric generator, the mechanical energy is produced by water turbines. These derive their energy from the enormous force of water flowing into them. This is regulated by sluice gates at the foot of the dam. The dam causes the water to build up behind it to a tremendous depth, thereby increasing its potential energy.

Turbogenerators are also driven by the force of waterfalls. Hydroelectricity is generated in vast quantities in mountainous countries where there are plenty of fast flowing rivers.

What is a transistor?

A transistor is a semiconductor device. It can be used to perform the same functions as a thermionic valve.

Semiconductors are a particular group of elements. They include carbon, silicon and germanium. Normally they are not good conductors, but it has been found that by adding a minute quantity of certain other elements, the conductivity of the semiconductors can be increased. In some, the addition of the impurities allows some of the electrons to move freely as in a metal. These are called n-type (negative) semiconductors. In others, the impurity creates a lack of free electrons so that positively charged particles appear to move through it. This is called a p-type (positive) semiconductor.

When a metallic conductor is heated its resistance increases as its temperature rises. In a semiconductor, however, the resistance decreases as its temperature rises; its conductivity rises and the electrons flow more freely. Semiconductors also differ from metallic conductors in that their conductivity is not the same in both directions.

Because of this ability to conduct freely in one direction only, semiconductor devices are used as rectifiers, in the place of thermionic valves.

A transistor is such a device. It consists of a sandwich of n-type and p-type semiconductors. It may be an n-p-n transistor or a p-n-p transistor. The three semiconductors are equivalent to the three connections in a triode valve, one being the cathode, one the anode and the middle of the sandwich is equivalent to the grid.

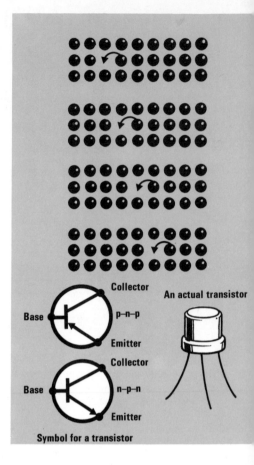

An actual transistor

Symbol for a transistor

What does 'solid state' mean?

Solid state physics is the study of matter in the solid state. The term solid state is also commonly used to refer to solid state devices. These are electronic devices such as transistors, semi-conductors and integrated circuits, that do not involve any moving parts, heated filaments or gases as valves do.

Solid state devices are very small and strong and can be mass produced cheaply. They are used in many items of modern equipment, from transistor radios to computers. Their small size has made it practical to build highly complex circuits which otherwise would have taken up an enormous amount of space.

Right: Modern electrical components can be made very small indeed.

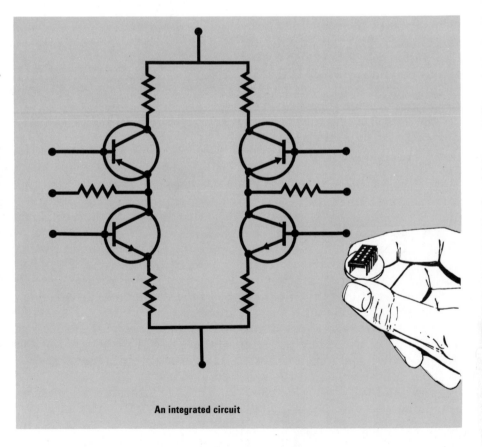

An integrated circuit

112

What is electrolysis?

A chemical reaction can produce an electric current by means of electrolysis. The solution in which such a reaction takes place is called an electrolyte. The current passes between two electrodes, from the positive anode to the negative cathode. Conversely, if an electric current is passed through an electrolyte by applying a voltage to the electrodes, it can cause a chemical reaction to take place.

This happens in the car battery. The chemical reaction between the lead plates and the sulphuric acid in the battery produces the electric current a car requires for its lights. By passing a current produced by the dynamo, in the opposite direction, the reverse of this chemical reaction takes place. This restores the electrolyte and the electrodes to their original chemical composition so that they can continue to react and produce a current.

Electrolysis is used for electroplating metal objects. To copper-plate an object, for example, it is suspended in copper sulphate solution, connected to the negative side of a battery. A second electrode is also connected, to the positive side of the battery, so that it acts as the anode, and is also suspended in the electrolyte. The current from the battery causes a chemical reaction to take place in which copper from the electrolyte is deposited on the cathode. The object becomes brightly coated with a layer of copper. If you look on the back of a piece of silver cutlery, you may see EPNS engraved in it. This stands for Electro Plated Nickel Silver. This type of silver is known as *plate* to distinguish it from solid silver.

What is a diode?

A diode is a thermionic valve (a radio valve containing a heated cathode). When a filament is heated it gives off, or emits, electrons, just as boiling water will give off steam. The hotter the filament, the more electrons are given off. These electrons have a negative charge and will be attracted to anything that has a positive charge. This behaviour is known as thermionic emission.

In a thermionic valve the air is removed. In this way a vacuum is left which allows the electrons to move freely. The valve contains a heated electrode, the cathode, and this emits electrons.

A voltage is applied to the valve so that there is a potential difference across it. Another electrode, the anode, is held at a higher potential than the cathode.

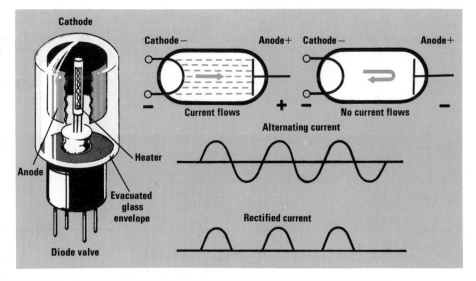

The negatively charged electrons are attracted to the positive anode.

Because the current only flows in one direction in a diode, it can be used to *rectify* an alternating current to direct current. It only conducts during one half of the current cycle.

Above: A diode can act as a rectifier, changing alternating current to direct current.

Why does one broken bulb make all the Christmas tree lights go out?

The lights on a Christmas tree will all go out if the circuit is broken. The current that flows through the wire and heats each bulb filament can only flow if it has a continuous closed circuit to flow round. If one bulb is broken, the circuit is broken at that point. To make all the bulbs light again, the broken one must be replaced, or cut out of the circuit by connecting up the wires on each side of it. But first it must be located. This means trying each bulb in turn, taking it out and replacing it with a new, good one, until, when the broken one is found, the replacement bulb makes them all light up again.

This problem only arises if the bulbs are connected in *series*; that is, wired together in one long chain so that the current passes through each one in turn.

If the bulbs are wired in *parallel*, the failure of one bulb will leave the rest lit because there is still a complete circuit for the current to flow round.

To wire the bulbs in parallel, they are connected across the

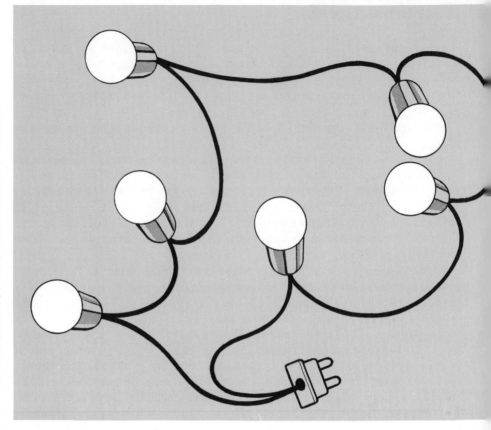

Above: Christmas tree lights are usually arranged in series.

two conductors leading from the battery. The result is rather like the rungs across a ladder. When one bulb breaks, the current can still flow through all the other bulbs or 'rungs'.

In a parallel circuit, all bulbs will receive the full voltage supplied to the circuit. They will therefore be brighter than those in a series, but the battery will not last as long, and a transformer would be needed to connect them to the mains supply.

Why does nylon crackle in the dark?

Nylon clothes sometimes can be heard to crackle and seen to produce small sparks and flashes because of static electricity. The effect is usually seen best in the dark.

The sparks are caused by an electric discharge that behaves like a miniature flash of lightning.

Artificial fibres such as nylon are particularly prone to building up a charge by the movement of electrons in their atoms.

114

Why does there seem to be more static electricity on dry days?

If you walk across a carpet and then touch a metal doorknob, you may hear the crack of a spark of electricity discharging. You may also feel a slight, stinging shock. In the dark you can see the spark. This is caused by the body building up a charge of static electricity, picked up from the fibres of the carpet. As you approach an object or person that is not charged up, the electric potential tries to discharge itself, jumping across the air gap before contact is made.

There are many common examples of sparks caused by static electricity discharging. These include hair crackling when it is combed, and nylon clothes crackling when you move or take them off.

All the effects happen more frequently and are more pronounced on cold, dry days. This is because the conductivity of the air is greater when there are only very few molecules of water vapour about, and when the air molecules are closer together because the temperature is low. Cold, dry air is able to pass a stronger spark of electricity across a gap than warm, damp air does.

Why does a balloon stick to the ceiling after rubbing it on your jumper?

A balloon can be made to appear to defy the law of gravity by making it stick on the ceiling. It is held there by the attractive force of a charge of electrons. The charge is built up by rubbing the balloon hard on a piece of wool, such as the sleeve of a sweater. This rubs off some of the electrons in the balloon rubber. The balloon has become positively charged because it has lost some of its negatively charged electrons. By this charge it is attracted to any free electrons in the fibres on the ceiling.

Various types of material can be charged up by rubbing them with certain other types. Sealing wax rubbed on wool, amber rubbed on fur or a nylon comb run through dry hair, will all attract small pieces of fluff or paper.

What is lightning?

Lightning is caused by a discharge of electricity, either between two clouds, or between a cloud and the Earth.

A flash or streak of lightning is in fact several sparks in quick succession. The eye sees them as one long streak. This type is known as forked lightning. There is also sheet lightning which is less dangerous.

The electric charge is built up by the breaking down of air molecules.

115

What does 'radioactive' mean?

Something that is radioactive gives off electromagnetic radiation of a very high frequency and short wavelength. This is because it contains certain types of atoms with unstable nuclei.

The nucleus of an atom is made up of protons and neutrons. All the atoms of a particular element contain the same number of protons, but they can contain different numbers of neutrons. Atoms of an element containing different numbers of neutrons are known as isotopes of an element. Certain isotopes are *unstable*; they emit radiation. These are known as radioactive isotopes or *radioisotopes*.

The most common form of radiation is called *beta particle emission*. A beta particle is an electron, but it is not one of the orbiting electrons from an atom. It is emitted from the nucleus where it is produced as a result of the disintegration of a neutron. The other products of this disintegration are a proton and a neutrino. The addition of another proton to an isotope changes it into the isotope of another element, since atoms of all elements always contain the same number of protons. This isotope may also be unstable and may disintegrate, or decay, further, to become another element. The decay continues until a stable isotope is formed. Throughout these changes beta particles are emitted.

Another common form of radiation is *alpha particle emission*. An alpha particle contains two protons and two neutrons. So the emission of an alpha particle changes a radioisotope to the isotope of an element with two fewer protons in its nucleus. Only the heavier elements emit alpha particles.

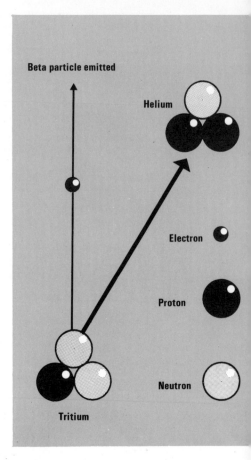

What is a geiger counter?

A geiger counter is an instrument for detecting radiation. It contains a gas which is held at low pressure. The gas surrounds a metal cathode cylinder, which has a thin wire anode running down its centre. There is a potential difference of about 1,000 volts across the electrodes. If any particles of ionizing radiation, such as alpha, beta or gamma rays, enter, the gas is ionized and there is a momentary current through the tube. This action produces a change in voltage which is amplified electronically to provide a digital read-out, or, in some instruments, it even lights a neon lamp or activates a loud-speaker.

Instruments that indicate levels of radiation are vital for people's safety. Radioisotopes are used in medicine to treat certain diseases, but the amount of radiation, the *dose*, has to be extremely carefully controlled. In some types of cancer, radiation is used to kill off the overactive cells. But an overdose of radiation could lead to vital organs being damaged.

People who work in radiation areas have to be screened from the radioactive source. Isotopes are handled by remote control and are stored in rooms and cases lined with lead. The streams of alpha and beta particles are absorbed by the lead, where they would pass straight through normal brickwork.

Portable geiger counters are taken to suspected areas where a radiation leak may have occurred, or where a source of radioactive material is discovered.

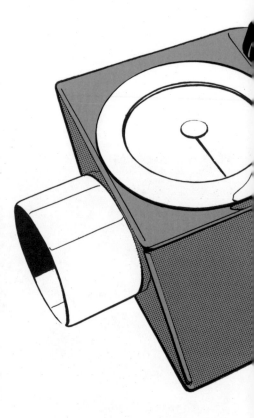

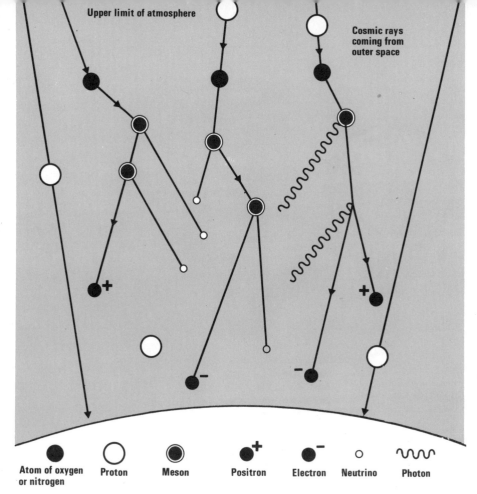

Upper limit of atmosphere

Cosmic rays coming from outer space

●	○	◉	●⁺	●⁻	○	∿∿
Atom of oxygen or nitrogen	**Proton**	**Meson**	**Positron**	**Electron**	**Neutrino**	**Photon**

What are cosmic rays?

Cosmic rays are very high energy radiation coming from outer space. Some come from the Sun, which is itself like a gigantic nuclear explosion, emitting high energy radiation all the time.

Cosmic rays strike the Earth continually from all directions, but fortunately the atmosphere prevents most of it from reaching the surface. The cosmic rays consist mainly of very high energy protons and alpha particles. Some of these collide with molecules of gas in the atmosphere, producing secondary cosmic rays and cosmic ray showers of *elementary particles*.

Cosmic rays have extraordinary penetrating power. They pass through not only the atmosphere, which is equivalent to passing through one metre of lead, but they also penetrate into the sea and underground.

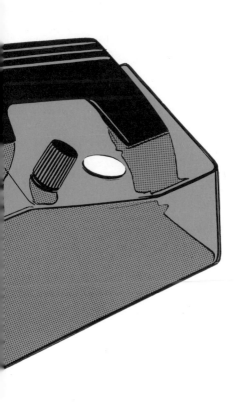

What is fall-out?

Fall-out is the radioactive matter which is deposited on the surface of the Earth from the atmosphere, after a nuclear explosion. There are three different types. *Local* fall-out consists of the large particles landing within 160 kilometres of the explosion. This takes place within the first few hours after the explosion.

Tropospheric fall-out is the deposition of fine particles which were carried up in the troposphere. It takes place all around the world, mainly in places at the same latitude as the scene of the explosion, and occurs within a few weeks.

Stratospheric fall-out continues for years. It is the deposition of fine particles of radioactive matter, blown up and carried in the stratosphere. It takes place all over the globe.

117

What is uranium?

Uranium is one of the Earth's most valuable, naturally occurring elements. It is a hard, white metal and is both the heaviest metal and the heaviest naturally occurring substance. Its great value is due to the fact that it is radioactive. Natural uranium contains 0·71 percent of the isotope uranium-235. This isotope can produce a nuclear chain reaction. It is used in nuclear reactors and nuclear weapons.

Uranium was the source of the first effects of radioactivity to be investigated. In 1896 the French physicist, Becquerel, found that some kind of emission from a lump of uranium produced an image on a photographic plate.

In 1940, scientists discovered that by bombarding uranium with neutrons, it could be transformed into heavier elements as it absorbed the neutrons. These elements are known as the *transuranic elements*. They include plutonium, thorium and curium. Curium was named in honour of Pierre and Marie Curie, who were the great pioneers of radioactive research.

How do we get nuclear energy?

Nuclear energy, or atomic energy, is released in nuclear reactors and nuclear weapons. It is released during a nuclear reaction where *mass* has been converted into energy.

Einstein's theory of relativity explains how mass and energy are really two different forms of the same thing. When the nucleus of an atom breaks up an enormous amount of *kinetic energy* is released. This is the energy of motion, and it is released because the particles in the nucleus move at tremendously high speeds when the atom is 'split'.

We obtain a useful amount of nuclear energy from a chain reaction. This is a continuous process in which the neutrons, emitted by the nucleus of one atom breaking up, cause the destruction of several neighbouring nuclei. This also leads to the release of more neutrons, and hence a continuous chain or *fission reaction*.

The initial reaction can be brought about by bombarding radioactive material with elementary particles. Some materials have to be enriched to keep a chain reaction going. The energy obtained from nuclear reactions has many uses. It can be converted into heat and used in power stations; several ships and submarines are already in service, powered by nuclear reactors, and it is also used in nuclear weapons.

What is nuclear fission?

Nuclear fission is a type of nuclear reaction during which the nucleus of an atom splits into two, releasing a vast amount of nuclear energy. Particles from the nucleus, known as neutrons, are also emitted. These will bombard the nuclei of neighbouring atoms causing them to split, starting a *chain reaction*.

Only fissile atoms will split when struck by a neutron. These atoms are relatively rare. The isotope uranium-235 is such a substance. It is found in very small quantities in natural uranium.

The enormous amounts of energy that are released during nuclear fission can be converted into heat and used as a source of power to drive engines and generators. The energy can also be put to a destructive use in nuclear weapons. In the atom bomb, all the energy of a fission reaction is released at once. The great dangers in this are not only the destructive force of the shock of the explosion. The contamination of the land and the atmosphere by the release of radioactive particles, known as fallout, also needs careful control.

The fission reaction in a nuclear reactor also has to be carefully controlled.

Fissile radioactive material is stored in small quantities of less than a certain amount, known as the *critical mass*. Below the critical mass, neutrons escape from the surface of the body of material, so there are not sufficient moving within the material to set up a chain reaction.

How does a nuclear reactor work?

Fissile material, such as uranium containing the isotope uranium-235, is used in a controlled nuclear fission reaction. It produces nuclear energy in a nuclear reactor, or creates more fissile material.

The atoms of the radio-active isotope split, releasing vast amounts of energy and emitting neutrons which bombard other fissile atoms, causing them to split. The rate of this chain reaction has to be very carefully regulated. To slow it down, a *moderator* is used.

In some reactors the fuel has to be *enriched* to make sufficient fissile atoms available. The great heat produced by the nuclear reaction has to be controlled by using a coolant.

In a *fast reactor* the fuel is enriched by increasing the proportion of the uranium-235 isotope in the fuel, or by adding another fissile element such as plutonium. Little or no moderator is used and the fast neutrons reach very high energy levels.

The *convertor reactor* converts fertile material into fissile material. Fertile material contains isotopes which can absorb neutrons and change into fissile isotopes.

In a *thermal reactor*, a moderator consisting of a neutral substance such as carbon is used to slow down some of the fast neutrons. As fast neutrons they would tend to be absorbed by uranium-238. As slow neutrons they are available to cause fission of the uranium-235 isotopes. This type of reactor generates heat which is extracted by a coolant and used to heat water. It can then provide steam to drive the turbines for electrical generators.

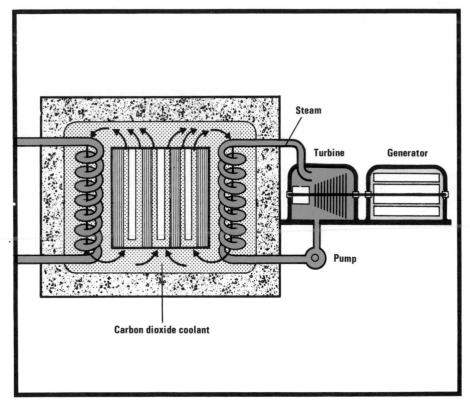

Steam

Turbine   Generator

Pump

Carbon dioxide coolant

What drives electric trains?

There are three main types of modern electric trains. Very powerful, diesel-electric locomotives pull the fast expresses in many countries. In these a diesel engine, run by oil, drives a generator which produces the electricity needed for the electric motors. These in turn drive the train and supply power to the train for heating and lighting.

The record for the fastest railway locomotive is held by a French electric one. It draws its power from an overhead wire through a strangely shaped frame called a *pantograph*. On some railways, a similar type of loco-motive draws its power from a *live rail*, which is a third rail placed alongside the track.

Multiple unit coaches have motors at the ends of each coach. This train is used on suburban and local services because the number of coaches which can be coupled together is flexible.

How does an electric motor work?

The principle of the electric generator is based on the fact that, if a conductor is moved through a magnetic field, a current is induced in the conductor.

The electric motor works on the converse principle. If a current is passed through a conductor which is situated in a magnetic field, the conductor will be made to move. In a simple motor, the conductor is a coil, the *armature*, which rotates between the poles of a magnet. This produces a direct rotational movement to the drive shaft.

Current is supplied to the coil through a *commutator*, which reverses the direction of the current. In this way the shaft is kept turning in the same direction.

Some motors run on direct current (d.c.); others run on alternating current (a.c.).

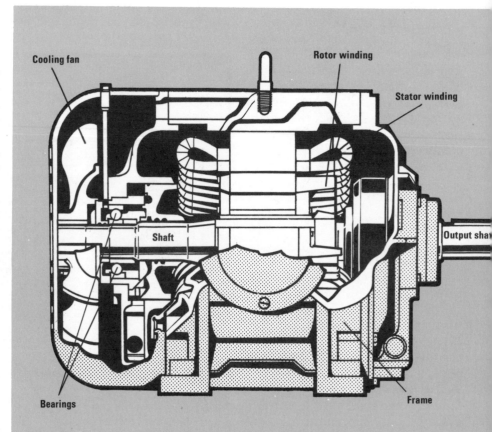

Cooling fan · Rotor winding · Stator winding · Shaft · Output shaft · Bearings · Frame

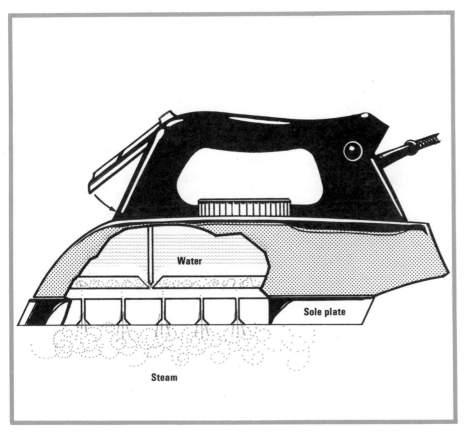

Water

Sole plate

Steam

How does a steam iron work?

It is easier to iron the creases out of cloth which is damp than when it is 'bone dry'. The steam iron is designed to dampen the cloth and iron out the creases all with one stroke.

The flat base, or sole-plate of the iron is made of heavy, highly conductive metal and is heated by an electric element immediately behind it. Next to the element are tubes containing the water which is heated to boiling point at the same time.

A switch makes it easy for you to release the steam when it is required.

The steam rises and comes out through several holes in the sole-plate. The sole-plate is also grooved, so that the steam flows along and dampens more of the cloth.

How does an electric convector heater work?

Convector heaters make use of natural convection currents to heat a room. Hot air rises because as the air is heated, it expands and grows less dense as the gas molecules move further apart. The lighter and less dense hot air rises and heavier, more dense, cool air is drawn beneath to replace it. These currents of air, called *convection currents*, are set up wherever the air is heated in one spot.

A convector heater contains an electrically heated filament enclosed in a case. It allows cool air to be drawn in underneath and heated air to rush out through the grill at the top.

A forced *convector heater* also contains an electric fan. This sucks cold air in and blows it across the elements to speed up the circulation of the air.

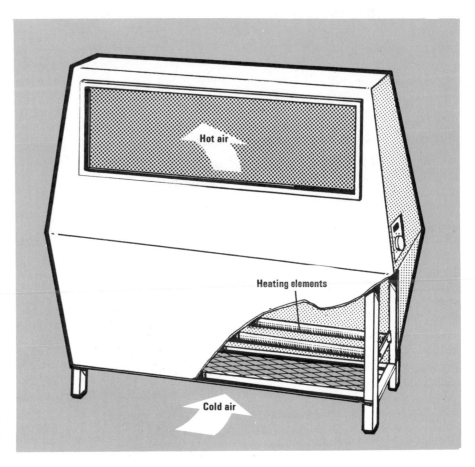

Hot air

Heating elements

Cold air

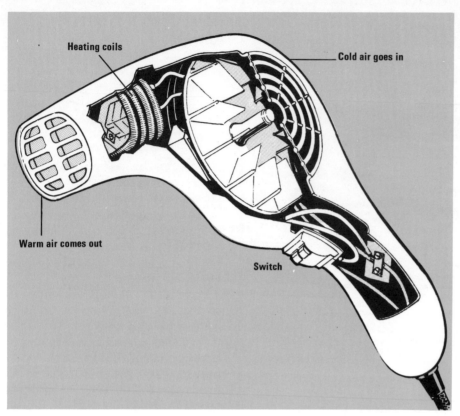

Heating coils

Cold air goes in

Warm air comes out

Switch

How does a hair drier work?

A hand-held hair drier gives out a jet of hot, dry air from a nozzle. This will very quickly make water evaporate from wet hair.

The air is sucked in by a small electric fan and is blown across the electrically heated elements. These elements then heat the air, which dries the hair.

Hair driers contain a thermostat, so that the air does not get too hot and singe the hair or damage the drier. The thermostat automatically cuts off the current from the elements if they overheat, if the air intake is blocked or if the fan stops. This is why it is so important not to lay the hair drier down and block the air intake. This intake is easy to find; usually it is the gridded section on the side.

Who invented radio?

Radio is a system in which electrical signals are sent from one place to another as electromagnetic radiation, instead of sending a current along wires—hence the name 'wireless'. Wireless telegraphy was invented by Marconi. In 1896 he sent a wireless message nearly 15 kilometres, and in 1901 he succeeded in transmitting a signal across the Atlantic, from England to Newfoundland.

Radio involves the transmission of electromagnetic energy in the form of *ground waves*. These follow the curve of the Earth's surface. The energy may also be in the form of *sky waves*, that are reflected off the electrically charged layer in the atmosphere, known as the *ionosphere*. The signal is sent out from a transmitting aerial and is picked up by a receiving aerial. Early radio signals were sent in *Morse Code*, by tapping a transmitting key.

Since the invention of the microphone and the electronic valve, it has been possible to convert sound into radio signals, providing us with the radio broadcasting systems of today.

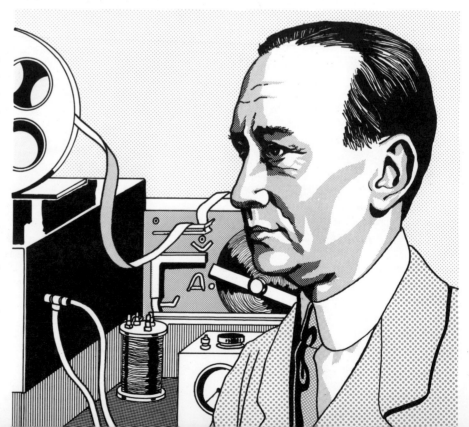

When was television invented?

The history of television is a long and controversial one. Over fifty years of research by scientists in many countries were involved in making it.

The cathode ray tube, which is the screen on which we receive a picture on our television receiving sets, was invented by Sir William Crookes in 1878.

The picture is built up on the screen, bit by bit, by the process known as *scanning*. The first mechanical scanning system was invented by Nipkow in 1884.

In 1923 Zworykin patented the iconoscope, which was the forerunner of the television camera. Later, he also demonstrated how a receiver works. Regular television broadcasts began in New York in the 1930s.

Meanwhile, other television systems had been worked on. In Britain, Logie Baird demonstrated his system, which worked by infra-red rays. He made successful transmissions in black-and-white and colour, and also across the Atlantic.

How is a TV picture produced?

The screen of a television receiver is coated with a fluorescent chemical which glows for a short time after being struck by an electron beam. This screen is at the end of a cathode ray tube, down which the beam is sent. The beam is made to flash across the screen from side to side, moving down slightly each time, covering the whole screen, or frame, in 625 lines. This process is known as scanning.

Each line forms part of the picture. The beam makes 30 frames per second. (The eye sees continuous movement after 12 pictures per second.) The electron beam is produced, after amplification, from the signal received from the broadcasting transmitter. At the same time a sound signal is received and the two are synchronized so that they are presented simultaneously.

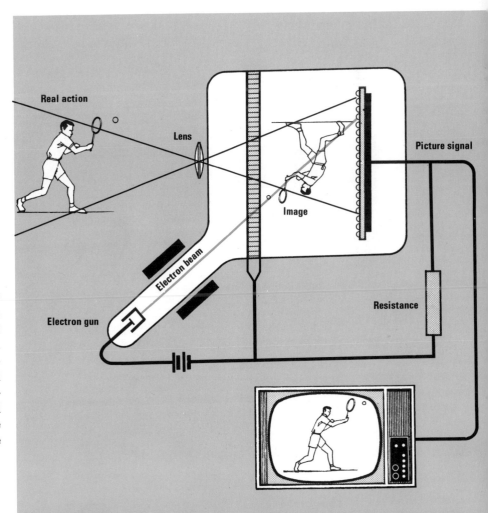

Real action

Lens

Picture signal

Image

Electron beam

Electron gun

Resistance

How is a TV picture transmitted?

The signal plate of a television camera is covered with thousands of light-sensitive dots. Light from the scene which is being transmitted falls on these dots and produces a signal which is picked up by an electron beam scanning the plate. The signal from the beam is amplified and is broadcast from the transmitter as *modulated radio frequency electromagnetic radiations.*

The signal is carried on a very high frequency carrier wave which travels in straight lines, unlike radio signals which can follow the curvature of the Earth. So the directional aerials that pick up the signal have to be placed high up, on housetops. A *relay transmitter* picks up the signal from the broadcasting transmitter and sends out, or relays, a stronger signal to places further away, where the original signal would have been too weak to pick up.

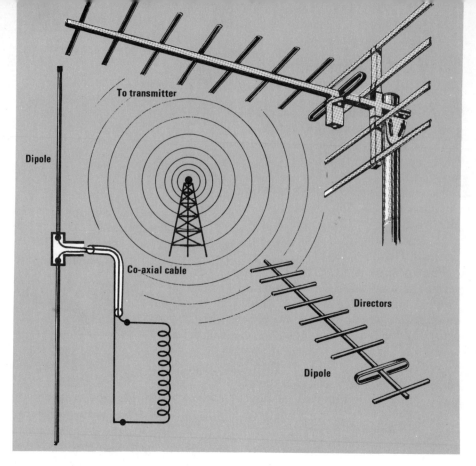

To transmitter

Dipole

Co-axial cable

Directors

Dipole

The sound and vision signals travel along co-axial cable, into the receiver set. Here they are amplified and changed into sound from a speaker and a scanning electron beam produces the picture that we finally see on the screen.

ACTION REPLAY

What is video tape?

Some television broadcasts are of live performances in which the signal from the camera is sent out immediately by the transmitter. Filmed recordings are also broadcast. A more direct method of recording television programmes, for transmission at another time, is on video tape. This is magnetic tape which contains information for both the audio (sound) and video (picture) signals, which are recorded on the same tape.

Video tape does not have to be processed like film, so is immediately available for playing back. It is used for action replay, and slow motion shots, which are especially popular in broadcasts of sporting events.

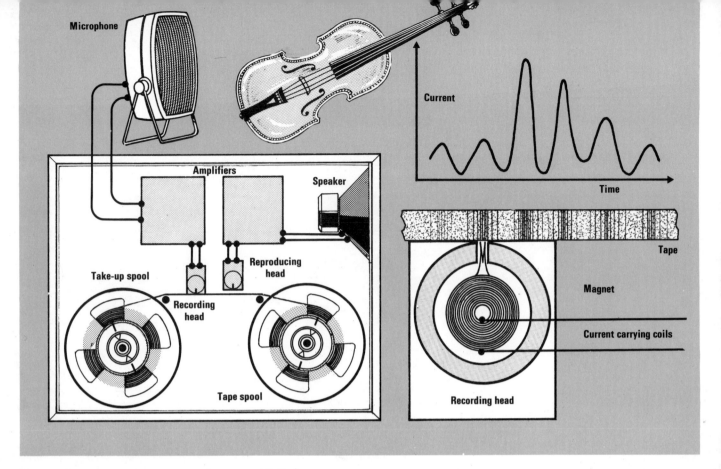

How does a tape recorder work?

Sound recordings are usually stored either on record discs, or magnetic tape. Magnetic tape is plastic tape, coated on one side with the metallic powder, iron oxide, which is magnetic.

When the magnetic tape is passed in front of an electromagnet, the iron oxide becomes magnetized, strongly or weakly, depending on the strength of the current in the electromagnet. The magnetized tape is then used to induce a current in another electromagnet.

The sounds to be recorded are picked up by a microphone which converts them into an electric current that varies with time. This current is amplified, which makes it stronger and shows up the variations more clearly. It is then fed to the recording head.

The recording head consists of an electromagnet made from a coil of wire, which carries the current, wound onto a curved iron core.

The magnetic tape is wound onto a spool and connected to a second, take-up spool. This is rotated by an electric motor, which can be driven at several constant speeds. As it is wound onto the take-up spool, the tape passes the recording head at a constant speed. The varying current in the recording head produces correspondingly varied magnetized sections on the tape.

To replay the recording, the direction of the tape is reversed and it is rewound onto the original spool. Then the tape recorder is switched to *play* and the tape moves past the heads once again. But this time the reproducing head is in operation. It is very close to the recording head and is similarly constructed. The moving magnetized tape induces a current in the reproducing head, which is the same as the original current produced by the microphone. This current is amplified and fed to a loudspeaker.